CASSIUS

THE TRUE STORY OF A
COURAGEOUS POLICE DOG

CASSIUS

GORDON THORBURN

JOHN BLAKE

Published by John Blake Publishing Ltd,
3 Bramber Court, 2 Bramber Road,
London W14 9PB, England

www.johnblakebooks.com

www.facebook.com/johnblakebooks ⬛
twitter.com/jblakebooks ⬛

First published in hardback in 2009
This paperback edition published 2010

ISBN: 978 1 84454 985 6

British Library Cataloguing-in-Publication Data:

A catalogue record for this book is available from the British Library.

Design by www.envydesign.co.uk

Printed in Great Britain by CPI Group (UK) Ltd

7 9 10 8

Papers used by John Blake Publishing are natural, recyclable products made from
wood grown in sustainable forests. The manufacturing processes conform to
the environmental regulations of the country of origin.

Every attempt has been made to contact the relevant copyright-holders, but some were
unobtainable. We would be grateful if the appropriate people could contact us.

To Laurie and Kelly

By the same author:

The Appleby Rai
Men and Sheds
Bombers, First and Last
Animal Spy
No Need to Die

ACKNOWLEDGEMENTS

... are, of course, due to the real Cassius, on whose life and times this book is closely based, and to his real handler, whose experiences in the British police force are here retold. The name and description of every person and place has been changed.

A man's dog stands by him in prosperity and in poverty, in health and in sickness. The one absolutely unselfish friend that a man can have in this selfish world, the one that never deserts him, the one that never proves ungrateful or treacherous, is his dog.

Senator George Graham Vest (1830-1904)
of Johnson County, Missouri.

Let me have men about me that are fat;
Sleek-headed men and such as sleep o' nights.
Yond' Cassius has a lean and hungry look;
He thinks too much: such men are dangerous.

I do not know the man I should avoid
So soon as that spare Cassius. He reads much;
He is a great observer, and he looks
Quite through the deeds of men.

William Shakespeare, *Julius Caesar*, Act I, Scene ii.

CONTENTS

CHAPTER ONE

PERHAPS SHE'LL DIE

For a January night on the edge of the moors, it could have been colder. Even so, she was more likely to be found dead than alive. The other possibility, more likely still, was nothing. The old girl had done this before – gone missing. Someone had rung the police that time saying there was an ancient and dotty lady on the bus to Clufford, a large northern industrial town, telling everyone she was meeting her fiancé, home from the war, and he'd be taking her for a stroll along the prom to see the pierrots.

On balance, thought PC Sleightholm, as he turned his van into the lane leading to the nursing home, it was not a promising job. This would be the first find-and-speak he and Cassius had done where the item to be found was not a car thief, burglar, armed robber or other criminal type. When Cassius found and spoke, bouncing on his front paws and showing his magnificent set of teeth, criminal types tended to stand still and tremble. If they didn't, Cassius bit them hard and ripped their clothes to shreds, as he was trained to do. This would not be quite the thing for a frail 96-year-old woman with angina and Alzheimer's. Finding without terrifying would be a challenge for both dog and man.

The bad news was that the nursing-home grounds had already been searched, three times. Any tracks the missing person might have left would have been confused with those of the staff, the two section officers who had answered the original call and two from Traffic who'd turned up as well. At least the other worst enemies of scent – strong winds and hot, drying sun – had not been operating, but the obstacles were still sufficient to defeat some dogs. Most dogs, even, muttered Sleightholm to himself. But not his Cassius, at that point sound asleep in the back of the van.

The grounds would be extensive, too, he thought, as his headlights picked out the enormous and fancy wrought-iron double gates between gateposts surmounted by stone lions couchant; then they revealed a wide shingle drive that took a long, gentle, spacious curve with, on either side, grassland leading to woods, then up to a pillared portico big enough to hold a board meeting. In the old days, he thought, there'd have been footmen to answer the door to the gentry while he, a common copper, would have gone around the back to the tradesmen's entrance.

A neat and tidy girl – a bit tubby, aged about eighteen, dark hair in a bun – opened half of the oak double doors and ushered the police officer into the hallway. Panelled walls, parquet floor, paintings up the staircase; if it hadn't been changed into a nursing home it would have to have been a country-house hotel. Or maybe a pop star would have bought it.

'Supper's over and cleared away,' the girl explained, 'so most of the staff have gone, and the manager. She was the one who called you. But I'll show you round outside if you like.'

Sleightholm politely declined the offer and went back to his van on the drive. A thin, hazy layer of cloud blocked most of the light from a half moon and, with curtains drawn, little help came from the house. Behind it there were vague shapes of buildings, a barn or an old cart shed, perhaps; to the front, open expanses sloping down to the lane, and trees, plenty of trees. He had no idea how far the grounds went. It wasn't a great estate, but there seemed to be enough of it to provide a thousand places for a small person to hide. Nursing-home owners like a lawn and a few sheltered spots for the residents to sit in the summer sun and, for a home as upmarket as this, a few quid could be added to the tariff for panoramic vistas across its own parkland to the valley below.

'Maybe there'll be bluebells in the spring,' mused Sleightholm to nobody as he opened the van door without much optimism. 'Come on, Cass,' he said, softly. The dog leaped out, instantly awake, eager as ever, anticipating, ears up, tail going. His master led him to a corner and said, 'Empty.' Obediently, on this occasion, Cassius lifted his leg.

The light breeze was south-westerly, so the pair of hunters made their way into it, to the wrought-iron gates. At the boundary, a high stone wall, Cassius was told to sit at his master's side. It made sense to divide the ground up and here was the obvious first area, to the left of the driveway: roughly half-and-half mown meadow and unkempt woods. The dog would need six or eight sweeps to check it out.

3

Cassius was on his toes, ready to go. Had it been an urgent, difficult search with a dangerous criminal at the end of it, Sleightholm would have geed the dog up a lot more. Here it was urgent and difficult all right, but the target was a small, fragile, possibly hypothermic old lady with a bad heart. That is, if she was still alive. Thoughts of Little Red Riding Hood went through the policeman's mind. Cassius, what big teeth you've got.

Cassius listened to his orders being whispered. Normally he would have heard, 'Hey you, this is the police, come out or I'll send the dog', twice, in a loud and threatening tone. Tonight, Sleightholm cut it down to one – 'Come out or I will send the dog' – and struggled to say those familiar trigger words in a quiet, soothing way. The second trigger followed almost by way of an apology. 'Where is he?' was almost inaudible. Even the wave of the arm in the desired direction was hardly demonstrative.

What? Cassius, like all good police dogs, was a conservative. He could adapt to change but that didn't mean he liked it, and yet again his master was asking something new of him, or at least the old familiar thing in an entirely new way. Still, he knew what was required and he was off, questing this way and that, his nose sifting through the thin layer of air just above the ground that would hold any remnant of the smell that shouldn't have been there, the smell that didn't fit, the smell that said 'follow me'.

Sleightholm stayed as close to the dog as he could, also looking with his torch, giving the odd prompt of 'Where is he?' but *sotto voce*. Any little alteration in Cassius's demeanour might show he was on to something but, for the first search, he was going through the motions and no more.

The pair went to another starting point on the opposite side of the drive. It was similar ground, grassland rising and falling, woods towards the boundary wall. Cassius went away with his usual enthusiasm, quickly decided there was no fun to be had here and came back, as if to say, 'OK boss, done that. Next?'

Sleightholm wasn't satisfied, snapped his fingers and pointed the dog back to work. Cassius looked, saw and went. When he tried to cut another corner, because he knew there was nothing there, his methodical master, who didn't know there was nothing there, redirected him with a 'Cass. Where is he?'

The main outbuilding was a tall stone carriage-house with archways and heavy wooden doors, built in times when standards were high. Beyond that was a range of single-storey stables, also stone. These had already been searched, of course, but by people, not by Cassius.

There was a car, a Morris Minor, on blocks in the high building, and a few bales of straw, miscellaneous sacks of something or other, a workbench, a few drums and cans and some garden tools. There was a ladder up to a hatchway in the floor above, which meant that Sleightholm had to go and have a look. His torch showed the loft to be completely empty, not that the old lady would have tried the ladder anyway.

There was a sudden kerfuffle below. Trying to shine his torch down, look down and climb down all at once, Sleightholm banged his head on the edge of the hatch. Bloody dog. What's the blasted…? The speed of Cassius's dash across the floor gave it away. Cat or rat. In here, rat.

'Cass! Aagh! No! LEAVE IT!' shouted Joe. He didn't care

about the rat's survival, but such a distraction set a search back to the beginning in terms of the dog's attitude. It was the wrong kind of excitement, as one of Joe's dog-school instructors used to say. Cassius, temptation behind him, came over to Joe with that look on his face. Rat? What rat?

Cats, hedgehogs and rats – and squirrels, which to a dog are only a kind of climbing rat – could try the discipline and training of any working dog. Joe could forgive his dog for chasing a rat. They were near impossible to resist. His father had kept ferrets and the family dog, a Cairn terrier, hated the ferrets with all the passion of a wee fighting Scot. He would sit in the garden, some yards back from the ferrets' cage, and stare into it, and at them, with a pure malevolence only superseded by his hatred of rats. When Sleightholm Senior took ferrets and terrier ratting in a farmer's barn, the two species forgot their differences in pursuit of a third: the common enemy. The ferrets would seek and find, and any rats running for it were snapped up by the terrier and had their necks broken in one shake. When the fun was over, ferrets and terrier would resume normal hostilities.

An hour had passed. If the old lady was here, she must surely be dead or very near it, and there was only one part of the grounds they hadn't covered. Behind the house was some wasteland with scrap materials laid about. To the right was a yard with piles of logs, rubbish bins, gas cylinders, all sorts of stuff. To the left there were patches of hard core, a few heaps of rubble, nettles, brambles, a door, some timber, some roof tiles, as if somebody had knocked down a couple of sheds and not got around to phase two of the project.

As Sleightholm sat Cassius down, he noticed that the wind had changed around to the south-east. A little gust blew directly in their faces. The dog raised his head and a charge of the right kind of excitement ran through him, as he smelled the smell that shouldn't be there. The policeman knew immediately, the instant he let the dog go, that Cassius had found. He clambered to the top of the biggest rubble heap and shone his torch where Cassius had disappeared into the darkness. The dog was hurtling along, flat out, arrow straight – towards what? Sleightholm could see a line of trees, presumably the boundary with the wall behind. Where Cass was heading there was no gate, no gap, no anything, just brambles and undergrowth, except... what was that? A silvery football?

Cassius stopped near the football and wagged his tail. Sleightholm bellowed, 'Down!'; the dog dropped, the policeman galloped like hell over nettles and dead bracken, and there she was. Sitting in a concrete culvert with a white-haired head poking over the top, dressed in a nightie and slippers with a lacy kind of dressing gown over her, was about five stone of very old lady.

The first call to the police had been at three in the afternoon. She had been there, in the cold, for six hours at the very least. Soon, she would have fallen into a coma. Without that dog, very shortly she'd have been dead. And how long before they would have found her body, in a culvert, out there on the wasteland where nobody ever bothered to go?

She looked up when Sleightholm arrived and smiled. 'Just a single, please,' she said. 'I'm meeting my fiancé, you see, so I don't know if I'll be coming back this way.'

CHAPTER TWO

A LEAN AND HUNGRY LOOK

Joseph Noel Sleightholm (born on Christmas Day) was a latecomer to the police, having set out to be an engineer and not getting into a job he really enjoyed until he was 27. Once in, he was drawn to dog-handling and spent some of his leave days happily up at the training school, mucking out and mucking in, feeling part of the camaraderie of a very exclusive club, being fleeced something rotten at lunchtime cards, and playing the part of the criminal who is chased and bitten by overenthusiastic hounds that don't have such opportunities as often as they'd like.

As a career move, to go for dog-handling was a big decision because it meant giving up promotion through the ranks, in uniform or CID. Career dog handlers were almost all career constables if they wanted to stay as operational coppers.

Another problem was the image dog handlers had at that time, in that particular police force anyway. You called them in, a van arrived, an Alsatian jumped out, sniffed around, had a pee and jumped back in again. Then came the revolution. A dog handler called Jack Robinson arrived and, before you could say, well, anything, he transformed the unit simply by being in it. From day one, stories were running around about him and his dog Jaffa, not a great name for a police dog but so called because he had an orange spot on his nose. He was not a fabulous looker from any other angle either, conforming to the Kennel Club breed standard only in the same way that the Bash Street Kids resemble Michelangelo's *David*, but he certainly had presence.

The standard GSD, the German Shepherd Dog – which some people wrongly call Alsatian (being a euphemism from the First World War when things German were not popular) – is black and tan. Jaffa was black and a mucky kind of grey. He was long in the leg, far too tall for a show dog, and his canine teeth were rounded at the ends, presumably from use. He didn't prance, or do the show-ring trot. He strolled, king of the street, 'nobody messes with me'. He had the swagger of the hard man, and everyone who saw, believed. Joe Sleightholm had recently passed his sergeant's exam, but half an hour of Jaffa changed his life for good.

Constable Joe, dreaming of Sergeant Joe, was on night duty in a section car when he had a call to attend at a big house in the country. The people were away and the alarm, linked directly to the station, had gone off. Thinking that it was probably the alarm that was faulty but there just might be a burglary in progress, Joe turned up the drive with his lights off and there was a van, a white Transit van, not the sort of vehicle you would expect to see in such a drive at such an hour. He left his police car blocking it as well as he could and crept around the back of the house, where lights were showing.

And there he saw something very few police officers are ever privileged to witness.

Standing at a very large sash window he looked in on a spacious drawing room, although it was more like a room in a museum than a room in a house. Well furnished with antiques and paintings, clocks, vases, and figurines on the marble mantle, it also contained several display cabinets. A housemaid's nightmare, thought Joe, as he watched two men inspecting the gear, discussing the merits of various *objets d'art*, putting some back where they'd been but packing others into a pair of large canvas hold-alls. It was like a scene from a play. They were quite well dressed, the men. Smart casual, you might say. They were not your usual downtown toe-rags looking for a telly and a few quid in cash.

Joe stared, fascinated, not quite knowing what to do next, when the decision was taken for him. The burglars must have sensed they were being watched because they turned, saw Joe looking through the window, put down whatever they were discussing at that moment, picked up the hold-alls and legged it through the far door. Joe set off after them, along the side of the house. Round the corner was a stretch of lawn, a vegetable garden and a high wall with a door swinging open leading to a lane and a field gate, also open. In the glimmer of the moon he could see his quarry well ahead of him. He chased, across a field with a mature crop of feed beans that kept tripping him up. They went around in a loop with the law gaining, ending back at the van. The villains were in it and starting the engine when a panting PC Sleightholm arrived.

Using tactics from the dodgems, they managed to squeeze past Joe's car but not before he'd truncheoned their windscreen into a concave spider's web and shattered the driver's side window entirely. Even so, they were away, with Joe leaping into his car, following and calling frantically on his radio for some assistance.

Unable to see properly through the spider's web, the two antique experts turned down a dead end and found the bottom of a ditch. Leaving their booty behind this time, they ran into the night, and Joe, arriving some minutes later, could see no point in looking for them. They could have gone anywhere. He was making his report when another vehicle drew up: a dog van. Out got Jack Robinson and Jaffa, who found the scent straight away and was off, with Jack a not very close second. Joe had to stay where he was, guarding the treasure and watching the burglars' Transit until the rota garage turned up to take it away.

A quarter of an hour went by. Joe thought he heard a dog bark. Another quarter of an hour and he saw a torchlight coming towards him, with two figures in front of it, silhouetted. He got his own torch and illuminated another scene from a play, or a film more like. The two silhouettes were the antique burglars, naturally, but what made Joe laugh out loud was the state of them. They looked like Worzel Gummidge on a stormy day, their clothes hanging in rags, their faces and bits of bare limb covered in mud, and with an air of utter defeat about them. Jaffa had done his job well.

Later, their protests of innocence were brilliant. *Van? Sorry. Nothing to do with us. We'd been out for an after-dinner walk in the moonlight and suddenly this ravening werewolf turned up and attacked us at random and we are going to sue.* The police proved it was the van they used for their day job as roofers, and Forensic proved that nobody else had driven it recently. *Ah well, yes, it was our van, and we were out scouting for a possible venue for lamping rabbits when, in an obvious case of mistaken identity, we were furiously pursued by a police car that forced us into a ditch.We'd thought the police might be armed, so we ran away, while the police smashed the windows and planted the hold-alls of stolen goods on us.* So, said Forensic, how come you have fragments of the smashed windscreen in your pockets?

They went down but, long before the court case – in fact, on the instant he saw the two ragged-trousered larcenists in his torchlight – Joe knew what he was going to do. Forget CID and Chief Superintendent. He had to follow Jack Robinson. With that key decision made, one-third of the team, the policeman, was ready. The other thirds were training/experience and the dog.

Sourcing dogs is a continual difficulty for the police. Some forces have tried breeding programmes but good parentage is no guarantee of good offspring, and there's the expense and staff needed to fill all that puppy time before the dogs are ready to start training. The combination of qualities required in a police dog – the nose, the biddability, the controllable aggression, the bravery, the talent for distinguishing the toe-rag from the good citizen, the fear-inspiring bark and looking the part – these do not necessarily come with any pedigree, nor do the genes predictably pass on.

On Joe's first training course, with both man and dog entirely lacking in experience, things went well but the dog had a secret:

a kidney disease. Already two weeks along the road, they found Joe another dog. The new partnership flew through the course, caught up on everything and graduated, with one problem: this dog would not find-and-speak. He would find, but refused to bark, even though he couldn't be dissuaded from barking most of the rest of the time.

Joe thought he could cure this difficulty. He would cure it, dammit, but the dog developed another bad habit; the police call it 'commuting'. He'd find, not speak, and run back to Joe all pleased with himself for finding, while the criminal got away.

They went back to school but nothing could be done. The dog was transferred to the prison service, where he would have a long and successful career, and Joe set off on his second full course with dog number three. This time it was the instructor who said no, three weeks in. This one seemed to need too much encouragement, too much reassurance that he was doing the right thing, and he didn't like barking unless the handler was beside him. There was a ready private market for dogs like this – German Shepherds obedience-trained by the police – which solved the dog's problem, if not PC Sleightholm's.

Another one looked promising, but no: too nice and friendly. The trainer knows how to manipulate and check a dog's mean streak, but the mean streak has to be there in the first place. One police handler had never lived down the time when his new dog, released on a search, disappeared entirely and, even with the help of other dogs and their handlers, could not be found. A woman rang the police a day later, saying she'd found this Alsatian wandering the streets and could she hand it in, please. It had been so dirty she'd given it a bath, and it was so nice-natured that if nobody claimed it, she'd like to take it herself.

Monday morning, start of the fifth week of a thirteen-week course, and Joe Sleightholm was dogless. The other five students clubbed together and bought him a nodding novelty dog for the back window of his car. Watching his colleagues work through the day, Joe felt himself getting towards the brink of giving up. One of the dogs in particular made him groan with envy: a handsome sable called Solo, silver-grey and black rather than tan and black, and the most natural trainee anybody had ever seen. Glen Conway, his handler, could hardly believe his luck, nevertheless maintaining to anyone who would listen that handlers always got the dogs they deserved. The names went around and around, thought Joe. Solo, Winston, Bruno, Nero, they came up all the time. A bit like border collies. They're all called Meg.

The other dogs on the course were generally average, good enough, but one, called Zero, had something distinctly evil about him. He bent his legs while working so his chest was almost on the ground. His handler, Dave Archer, called him 'the snake in the grass'. Joe would have given his all for any one of them, but he couldn't, he was bereft, and the inspector's exam suddenly seemed so much more attractive. He had an engineering HND. He could study, get to Bramshill police college, and soon find himself in an office where people called him sir, where he could sit and get on the radio to turn out these bloody dog handlers and send them off into the hills and dales in the cold and wet.

That evening, with the dogs fed and watered and put in their kennels, the talk as usual turned to the finer points of long down, open-wood search, property square and irretrievable articles, or at least to the preferred place for such talk.

'We were at the Italian two nights ago,' said one.

'What about the Happy Moon? I know it was crap last time…'

'Joe, what do you think? You've said nowt.'

'I don't mind,' said Joe. 'Anything.'

'Hey, come on, Joe. It'll be all right. They'll find you a dog. I hear they're bringing in a Lhasa apso for tracking down people's escaped pet mice. Oh, sorry Joe. Sorry, mate.'

Joe was looking rather wet-eyed and not entirely suitable for piss-taking. A few seconds' uncomfortable silence was broken by Biro the instructor charging in, as usual opening the door as if expecting to brush aside whatever dead bodies and sacks of coal there might be lying behind it. He was called Biro by everyone, including the most senior officers in the force, because he was very tall and very thin with a perfectly round and shiny ball where his head should have been.

'Right, lads,' he declared. 'I want you back in good time tonight, and up early to get your jobs done in the morning. We've got an extra message to run. We're going to see a man about a dog. So, over the next hour or two, if you can spare a moment from ogling barmaids and waitresses, you can work out how we can all help Joe catch up five weeks with his new dog.'

The standard dog-school day started a few minutes before eight. Every handler washed and disinfected his own dog's kennel and, if they were short on pre-school induction trainees (otherwise known as those on the shit-shovelling course), everyone would help the permanent staff with the boarders.

Sometimes there might be fifty dogs there – potential, current and ex – including bomb dogs (usually Labradors) and cash dogs and drug dogs (usually spaniels). Grooming was next, when the dogs stood with their front paws up on the grooming blocks and luxuriated in the attention and the massage. Every man on that course, and every other course before or since, had somehow acquired an old handbag from a WPC (a) to keep his grooming gear in and (b) to make an excellent training aid for retrieving. Female handlers on the course had to provide their own handbags.

Joe Sleightholm was there, in among it, and was as ready as the rest for the nine-o'clock brew, served this morning at a quarter to. His excitement was intense. New dog. New dog! Biro would not be leading him on another fruitless journey. If he was, this would surely be the last stop.

The rest of the students would be on moorland tracking that day, but they all came with Biro and Joe to see the recruit. On the way, Joe restated his preference for the short-haired model of GSD. They didn't make such a mess all over the place when they shook.

'Where are you taking us, Biro?' said Joe.

'Gun-dog kennels,' came the economical reply.

'Gun-dog kennels? What are you going to give me, a red setter?'

'No, lad. Not a setter as such. You see, in my capacity as your revered leader and figurehead, I've got you a new job. A nice little number attached to HM Customs: sniffing suitcases for genetically modified vegetables.'

'Let's hope it gets me off the backward bobbies' course anyway,' said Joe.

Biro smiled at Joe's self-mockery. 'Backward bobbies' was the name they gave to the force's special course for older police officers, to get them up to speed on the new technology.

They drew up beside something that looked like a small, very well-kept prison camp. There were large wooden huts, tall fences with strong steel mesh, everything neat and tidy and implying no expense spared. The sign outside the kennels announced Greenwood Labradors, with a painting of a black lab and two shotguns crossed.

'They breed them,' said Biro, as they disembarked and walked across to the fence. 'Cracking bomb dogs, they make.' Before Joe could get another protest out, appearing from nowhere, the largest, longest-haired German Shepherd he'd ever seen bounded across the yard, put his paws up against the fence and gave them what for. What a bark. What a set of teeth. Here was a dog with bottle.

A girl appeared next, a slip of a thing, blonde, pretty, five-foot two, only about sixteen or seventeen. 'Cassius,' she said, firmly. The dog immediately shut up, trotted to her and sat by her left side. She threw one of the dummy birds they use for gun-dog training. The hairy monster ran for it, picked it up, ran back, dropped it at her feet, looked up at her and wagged a very large and brushy tail. She walked around the yard, about-turning, faster, slower, twisting, back again, this way, that way, and the dog, not on a lead, never left her side and never took his eyes off her. Joe was smitten.

'Apparently,' said Biro, 'he was all right with the family who had him, but he wouldn't let anyone else near the house. Wealthy people, big place, but even with him locked up they couldn't get a baby sitter. And they had to collect their post. So what I thought we'd do is give them your last one, the one that was too nice, and we'd take Cassius. Eighteen months old. Top of the age limit. What do you think?'

Joe Sleightholm knew precisely what he thought. He thought that the gods of dogs and police officers had combined to bring him the best animal ever, anywhere, in the history of the universe. The petite kennel maid came through the gate with Cassius, took the check chain and lead from Joe's hand, put it on the dog and passed him over into police custody.

'He'll always be a bit of a risk,' she said, looking up at the six-foot-three copper from waist height. 'Intelligent, wants to learn, wants to please, but excitable. Very strong, seems to have a good nose, but liable to forget his manners occasionally. Expect a nip or two.'

'Why, has he nipped you?' asked Sleightholm.

'Oh no,' replied the girl. 'He wouldn't bite me. I wouldn't stand for it.'

Joe walked Cassius up and down while Biro filled in the forms. All reservations about long hair and shaking mess were forgotten. Joe had loved the dog at first sight. What Cassius might think about it was not yet clear, but he seemed to be no problem on the lead. If that kennel maid were taller, thought Joe, she could join the police and be that relative rarity, a female dog handler. She'd probably be the instructor inside a week.

The big van, a police minibus with cages in the back, could

accommodate six dogs. There were five in there already, three on the top row, two below. Biro opened the van door and all five started barking when they saw the new boy, sitting quietly beside Joe. Biro unlocked the cage and gestured his 'come on in, you're welcome' with a dramatic bow and a wave of the arm. Cassius looked at Joe, Joe let go of the lead and in leaped the dog.

'I think he'll do,' said Biro as he closed up the van. 'I think he'll do.'

At the car park on the moors, they split, Cassius and Joe to the north, everybody else to the east. For the new pairing, this was getting-to-know-you time. It was a brisk, grey sort of a late February day, cloudy but good visibility apart from the odd snow flurry, and Joe felt his spirits rise as the two of them set off up a farm track and on to the open hills. He chattered away to the dog, mentioning the name from time to time, marvelling at the dog's immaculate behaviour and increasing his respect even more for that little kennel maid.

They must have walked for half an hour, stopping sometimes for Joe to stroke Cassius's flank, before the dog forgot himself and pulled on the lead. Joe was so surprised that instead of the orthodox tug on the chain and the command of 'Heel', he shouted 'Oi!' Without looking up, Cassius did a kind of four-footed reverse chassé, ended up exactly where he should have been and walked on in serenity. Joe felt moved to stroke the dog's ears and the massive main of creamy-coloured hair that flowed down his shoulders.

This dog was enjoying life. No doubt he'd been mostly kept in at his original home, and the kennels, comfortable as they were,

were still a confinement. Here he was in the open – a dog in the big, wide world – and now came Joe's first real test. He let Cassius off the lead.

Nothing remarkable happened. The dog trotted ahead, lifted his leg, had a good sniff around for general information, trotted on, lifted his leg again, and stopped, and looked and raised his nose a little. There was something in the air outside his ken. The moorland wind, no more than an icy nuisance to Joe, had some codes in it that needed to be absorbed and sorted – over there. 'Over there' consisted of many square miles of star moss, peat, puddles, grass tussocks, patches of heather and bracken, sheep runs and remnants of dry-stone walls. It was another key moment.

'Cassius,' Joe called. The dog turned and came back. 'Good lad, good lad, Cass.' They walked some more. Before two hours was up, Cassius was retrieving a ball and it was difficult to tell whether dog or man was the happier. They came down off the moor, met the road and turned towards the car park. Behind a fence was Biro, waiting for the others. He'd been the hare on a continuation track, where the dogs took it in turns to follow his scent, like a relay.

He made rabbit ears at Cassius, and stuck his tongue out. The noble hound stopped and stared in disapproval. Biro waved his hands in the air, performed a couple of crazy star jumps and went into a routine that would have been a credit to Uncle Eric doing a rain dance at the post-wedding disco.

Had Cassius not been on the lead, that would have been Biro's last dance, no matter how high the fence. As it was, the dog was on his back legs, barking like fury, lips curled back, teeth seeking blood as he protected his companion Joe against the threat posed by the gyrating madman. Biro laughed.

'Good dog, that,' he said. 'And when you get your commendations and whatnot in the future, just you remember who found him for you.'

The other dogs jumped into their cages and the men climbed into the van for lunch, except Joe. He took his ham sandwiches and Cassius to the other side of the car park, out of the wind, and they dined together. The dog had never had a morning like it in his life. A long walk across the moors, games of ball and now ham sandwiches with a new friend; things were looking up.

Sandwiches finished, flask emptied, legs stretched, Biro came over to suggest they try a little tracking. Police definition: 'To search to find, and then to follow, a particular track to its conclusion and to indicate anything along that track that is relevant', which was too tall an order for a dog with about three hours' service, especially the 'indicate' part. While the rest of the course went off to do a few exercises, Joe got the harness from the van and started to fit it on Cass. The first problem was adjusting it. Every buckle and strap had to be let out. There was a big frame and a heavily muscled body under all that hair. There was no second problem, though. A lot of dogs would have struggled and tried to wrestle their way out of such new restrictions, but Cass didn't mind the harness. He'd liked every surprise and innovation so far in the day; maybe he thought this would lead to another bit of fun.

It's natural for a dog to look for something with its nose rather than its eyes, but following a track is a skill that has to be learned.

A wild hunting dog will seek here and there, crossing and re-crossing a prey's track while progressing in the general direction, realising that here was the scent it wanted but not understanding that the track was a direct short-cut.

With Cass fully fitted and Joe holding tight to the running cord, Biro stood in front of them, a few feet away, and flapped a piece of old rag towards the dog's nose. Cass barked his irritation. With some ceremony, Biro turned and set off through the grass, shuffling his feet and waving his rag like a morris dancer who's lost one of his hankies. Cass watched with great interest and pulled against Joe's grip. This was a new game, it would surely be a good one, but the dog didn't know the rules yet.

At about thirty yards out, Biro did a pirouette, made a show of hiding the rag in the long grass with a grand flourish, and shuffled back with his hands spread open and empty. As he passed, Joe said 'Seek' firmly and loudly, and let the eager dog go, paying out the cord as fast as he could. Cass ran, head down, doing exactly what the wild dogs do – zigging and zagging, not clicking on to the fact that a thin line of mixed scents including boot polish, crushed insects, broken grass stems, metal and oil from the van and the spilt coffee Biro had trodden in that morning, would take him straight to the pot of gold, or piece of old rag.

With a new dog, a first timer, Joe had expected that encouragement would be needed. A dog might do a bit, cast around a little, and give up or be distracted by another interesting smell. Cass needed no persuasion. He found his rag trophy inside twenty seconds. Joe shrieked his approval, wound in the cord as he trotted up, and made a huge fuss of Cassius.

The first triumph of the probationary police dog Cassius required a bigger reward than pats and 'Good lads, so Joe grabbed one end of the rag and pulled. Cass was on to the ancient game of tuggy immediately; you wouldn't do it with gun dogs, because it hardens their mouths, but Cass's purpose in life was not to retrieve pheasants without fracturing a feather. The harder his mouth could be, the better, and tuggy was a terrific game.

Judging when enough was enough, Joe said, 'Leave', and let go the rag. Probably through sheer surprise, Cass dropped it too. Joe swept it up and put it in his pocket before the dog could change his mind, and there was praise and another track to be set by Biro: 30 yards of scuffling, followed by the same sequence of events from the dog on the command 'Seek': questing, finding, praise, tuggy, leave. Cass didn't want to leave it, because that meant his friend wouldn't play any more.

Joe turned his back, walked away a few steps, turned and said, 'Leave', very firmly. No go, and it took several more mini-confrontations before Cass got the true message. Contrary to his instinct, if he didn't leave there would be no more games. Eventually, leaving would be so automatic that Joe would be able to give the toy back for more tuggy and let the dog win, so he could shake whatever it was and kill it. He wouldn't be doing that today, but what about the tracking? Would he do that?

They ran another track, 30 yards criss-crossed and zig-zagged again, and another, and another, then the dog had his revelation. The penny dropped. He stopped being a wild dog and became a civilised one. He followed the final ten yards or so in a straight line, on the track as laid. It was only half a cricket pitch, but by

George he'd got it. The line of scents would take him directly to his reward. He'd tracked on his first lesson, without indicating relevancies, but that didn't matter at this stage. That would come later. It had been a new track, so easier with no time for the scents to weaken or be blown off course, like smoke from a chimney in a wind. Regardless of all that, the point was that Cassius was a genius. Wasn't that right, Biro?

CHAPTER THREE

THEY'VE NEVER DONE THIS BEFORE

On the drive back, Joe found himself in grave danger of incurring a fine for being boring, so full of it was he. This dog was the best, was going to be the best, would soon be the best. Cassius, the wonder dog. If his colleagues hadn't made allowances for him over such a lot of set-backs in the last five weeks, PC Sleightholm would surely have been looking forward to buying all the beer that evening and probably the Bangalore phaal as well, at The Garden of Death, as the local curry house was known.

The noise and bustle of the dog school at feeding time might have proved rather too exciting for Cassius, especially as he didn't seem to like his fellow students much, so Joe put him on the lead and walked him across the parade ground to the grooming blocks – long wooden beams set on concrete plinths about thigh height to a man. Placing the dog's front paws on the block, Joe began brushing the school's longest-coated undergraduate.

There are few things a dog likes more than being brushed, and Cass loved it. He didn't even complain when Joe did his tail. If only sports teams and groups of management trainees could bond as well as a man and his dog. Part of the way through, Dave Archer, handler of the snake in the grass aka Zero, wandered over to see how things were going. He put his hand out to give Cass a sniff, to mark him as friend, and very sharply withdrew it when the dog tried to remove all the fingers in one mouthful.

'Bloody hell, Joe,' said Dave, 'you've got a job on there.'

'I know,' said Joe, smiling broadly. 'Aren't you jealous?'

The dog school was another place a little like a prison camp, with admin blocks and kennels arranged around two sides of a high-fenced parade square. The kennels were in rows of eight, about six feet high so people could walk in and out easily, runs roofed with corrugated plastic, with metal grid gates, floors sloping gently to the front for drainage tiled in beige, and walls tiled in red. The front room, as it were, the run, was about six feet long, and sleeping quarters at the back were separated by a wall with a hatch at floor level and a small window higher up. In this back room was a raised platform that the dog could sleep on if it wished. Each kennel had boards placed so that no dog could see another. A bucket of water completed the furniture of these spartan lodgings, to which Joe now introduced Cass, while he went to get the dog's dinner.

The kennel staff would normally prepare the food in a numbered bowl, but Cass wasn't a checked-in resident yet. The choice was: complete dry meal, or tins with biscuits, or raw meat with biscuits. Joe opened two tins of Chum, added the Winalot, and took it to his guest, hoping that he'd made the right selection.

'Cass,' he said, 'one day, when you're trained and living at home, you'll be fed on complete dry stuff, because I hate opening tins, with the occasional mackerel, grilled of course, and scrambled eggs. You'll have tripe from time to time – we've got a very good butcher's on our street – and a big beef knuckle bone once a week, and a drop of cod liver oil for your joints.'

Cass didn't seem to care and never would. If it was food, he'd eat it. Although, given the choice, he'd probably go for raw mince and biscuit, with a warm kipper on Sundays.

After dinner there was the traditional short walk to the school's private park, an area of trees and grass known as Shit Wood. Cass's attitude to the other dogs had already made Joe wary, but they were alone in the wood so Cass could roam. While the dog snuffled among the dead leaves, chewed a stick, did his business and generally larked about, PC Sleightholm contemplated his good fortune. That there was something special about this animal was a fact obvious to everyone. It was also clear that those qualities which made him special would also make him difficult to curb and keep in good discipline. No art without work, thought Joe. 'Come on Cass,' he said aloud. 'Time for bed.'

Next morning, Joe was decidedly nervous. The dog had been used to kennels so confinement for the night wouldn't have been a worry. No, what would matter was if Cass recognised Joe as friend and master, saw him as something continuous and stable in what had recently been a topsy-turvy life and, above all, if there was any pleasure in it. Before he got as far as Cass's kennel, Joe was accosted by one of the kennel staff.

'That new dog of yours,' she said. 'Me and Sarah went to see him. What a handsome beast, but I'll tell you what. You won't find many in this school who'll go in with him.'

Joe hurried on. It's fine for police dogs to be anti-criminal, anti-riff-raff, but you don't really want them to be anti-social entirely. It would make life difficult if Cass in a kennel was like the dog in the manger, refusing permission for anyone except Joe to do anything like fill his water bucket.

Except Joe? Maybe Cass had already forgotten about yesterday and his friend. Maybe he thought his spartan cell was his new reality and his two-yard run his new world. Maybe that was why he'd blown up at the kennel maids.

Joe had to hope that Cass was simply a very territorial dog. Whatever he had, wherever he was, it was his and no person and no animal was going to trespass against him. If that was the case, it could be worked around, but life would become impossible if he had a foul and unpredictable temper, if he had a screw loose, if that trainer at the gun-dog place had been understating it when she said Joe should be prepared for the odd nip.

The run was empty when Joe got there. Cass was in the back, in his night cell. Joe rattled the cage door, the dog shot out of the hatch, barking like fury, and stopped the instant he saw who it was. Joe opened the door, Cass wagged his tail and the sun was shining again. Off they went to Shit Wood.

There would be other dogs there, and other police students, so Cass was kept on the lead, which was just as well because he had a go at the first dog he came across. This dog, loose, came up to say hello and got a ferocious welcome and a bite on his neck for his trouble. Still, he was a potential police dog like Cass and he wasn't going to give in easily. Immediately they were scrapping at full volume. Pulling on Cass's lead only put him at a disadvantage and did nothing to separate them, but the second dog's handler was soon there and the two coppers could end the fight in the time-honoured way. Joe got hold of Cass's tail as near the body as he could, the other cop did the same to his dog, and they heaved. Both dogs turned to see what was happening to their rear ends, ready to bite whatever it might be; the handlers grabbed them by the scruff and turned them away from each other. Problem solved, although it's a procedure always needing a certain amount of nerve and decisive action. He who hesitates is bitten.

The general routine was thus established that first morning. All the handlers except Joe would congregate at the usual clearing in the woods, where they had a chat and a smoke while their dogs footled about and hopefully did what they came for. Joe, and Cass on the lead, would go to the far side of the wood, in splendid isolation.

It was mucking out time. Joe put Cass in the backroom and slid down the hatch, wondering if he'd ever be able to leave this dog, like some did, lying down to command outside the run while he flushed it out with boiling water and disinfectant. Probably not.

Another problem, assuming Cass graduated and came home, would be when Joe was on leave and had to board his dog back at the school. Who would get him out to walk him? Who would go in to retrieve his empty dinner bowl? Was he going to be such a one-man dog that he was impossible for anyone else to deal with?

After mucking out, it was grooming time. At least the sheer enjoyment of that was enough to keep Cass's mind off other dogs and, soothed, he could be returned to his sparkling clean run while Joe went off for his morning brew in the locker room.

The social centre of the school was that locker room, off which opened the drying room and the lavatories. The table in the centre served as a bench for cleaning leather harnesses and leads. At busy times there could be a General Purpose Dog (GPD) initial course, a GPD advanced course, Bomb Dog courses, Drug Dog, Body Dog and Cash Dog courses. Other police forces in the UK that didn't have their own school (and police forces from all around the world, for that matter) sent students. The students' common denominators were generally a good arrest record and a certain humorous gregariousness that seemed to go with those who wanted to be dog handlers. PCs and WPCs from Devon and Suffolk could find themselves mixing freely with Colombian police who came to be trained and to take home British drug dogs, and who were famous in the locker room for eating the red bits out of the bones of the chicken legs that sometimes enriched their school-issue lunch boxes.

One Brazilian was a massive fellow who would not believe that his spaniel, from floor level, would be able to detect drugs on a high shelf and that, when it did, would indicate with an excited, head-up pose. This colossus of Rio would therefore lift the little dog in his pit-shovel hands and poke its nose into high places, and so he never could tell if it was indicating or not.

An inspector from Singapore didn't think that mucking out kennels was the accepted thing to do for one in his situation, he being of the officer class, and insisted on the work being subcontracted to lesser mortals. It was pointed out that this was an opportunity for the handler to check on his dog's health. He knew what went into the dog and, by the look of what came out, there might be hints of sickness in the animal. Oh, that was all right, the inspector had chaps back home who would write him a daily report on such matters.

Germans, French, Italians, Mexicans, Australians, anyone could be there; from the Detroit Police Department K-9 Unit to the St Petersburg Bomb Squad to the Sri Lanka Customs Office, and they'd mostly have been out on the beer the night before. The combination of aromas – sweat, damp clothes and boots, leather polish, yesterday's garlic and Guinness, this morning's toothpaste and aftershave – made for a locker room of legend, a place in which memories were imprinted, mickey was extracted, friends were made and hangovers suffered.

Anyone new would be taken out to the hallway and shown the glass case on the wall containing the preserved skeleton of a German Shepherd dog. 'This is the one we trained not to eat,' said the guide, offering up a comedy gem that might have to be translated into Romanian or Vietnamese (whereupon it could lose some of its original sparkle). The overseas students often brought their own interpreters, whose main role was in translating jokes in pubs and elsewhere. What three things do you need to run a police station? A computer, a police officer and a dog. The computer does the work, the dog prevents the officer going anywhere near the computer and the officer feeds the dog.

Interpreters' other duties included being intermediary between instructors and students out on exercise. The result was a comical scenario in which instructors issued commands in English, the interpreters translated, and the students reissued the commands in their own language. The dogs never seemed to have a problem with this.

On Cass's first morning of catching up, some of the students were off on the moors, some were performing in the training field where the agility equipment and jumps were, bbut the General Purpose Dog initial training course had graduated from straight lines, knowing where the track started, to the track box, a track laid along an imaginary 20-yard square marked by four poles in the corner of a field, meant to represent a building and so the starting point for a felonious track that could lead out and away to anywhere. Biro told them to set some tracks for each other then go for an extra brew while the tracks were cooking. He wanted a little time with Joe and Cass solo, and it was far too early for them to be thinking about track boxes.

The farmer who owned the surrounding land was happy to let the school use it, provided they didn't interfere with the agricultural seasons. Just now was ideal for novice tracking. The grass was fairly well grown from its last silage cut the previous summer and the livestock hadn't been let out of winter quarters yet. The worst conditions were newly mown, very short grass in the August noonday sun with a strong breeze. Joe and Cass had a still, overcast day on wet grass that was long enough to leave footprints, so the handler could see when the dog was going wrong.

As they strolled to the field, Joe let Cass run on ahead. 'Look at his gait, Biro,' said Joe. 'His hips. He walks like Marilyn Monroe. You don't think it's dysplasia, do you?'

'More of a Jane Russell I'd say, or maybe Jayne Mansfield. Did you ever see that film, *The Girl Can't Help It*? There's a scene in it of Jayne Mansfield going up some stairs, filmed from behind. Behind being the operative word.'

'Before my time, Biro. And what about Cass's hips?'

'Nothing wrong with his hips. If it was dysplasia he'd be in pain. He's not in pain, he's not trying to avoid strenuous exercise. Nothing wrong with his hips. Mind you, if we put him in for X-ray they'd probably say he wasn't right. But that's vets for you. He's a bloody good dog, Joe. He'll do well for you.'

Biro began with a repeat of yesterday, a dramatically obvious shuffle in a straight line, 20 yards, a big gesture with the rag and a shuffle back. Cass was straining at the harness. He knew this game. He wanted to be at it. Joe wondered if Cass would retain the trick he'd learned about precision, that the track led to the prize, or if they'd have to start again from pure instinct. Joe needn't have worried: Cass was a natural. Head sharp down, body weight leaning into the harness; everything about his line and shape said that he was in business. With Joe paying out line as quickly and smoothly as he could, Cass ran along the track without hesitation or deviation, straight to the rag, which he picked up and shook. He ran a few bounds to one side and shook it again. The rag had to die.

'Good boy, Cass!' yelled Joe, having decided to use the full or 'Sunday' version of the name only when he was displeased, and ran to his dog. The dog stopped shaking the rag, looked at Joe, trotted over to meet him and sat with it in his mouth. Fuss and tuggy were Cass's reward, then 'Leave', rag in pocket, walk together back to the start of the track, hand rag to Biro, walk over to a virgin stretch of grass and repeat for a bit longer this time.

Another track, longer still, and another, and the dog was in a groove. Some of the other course members were out now, watching from a discreet distance. The subtleties of inter-student competition might entertain the conversation in the pub – how it was a greater achievement to train a less-talented dog, how two perfect long-downs were worth more than one perfect property-square – but the best handler with the best dog was just that: the best. Joe would never, never have claimed to be the best handler (well, hardly ever) but he was increasingly convinced that his dog was a nonpareil, and some of the other students were thinking the same way.

Cass was finding the trophy, enjoying the tuggy, letting Joe take it when asked to leave and giving the impression of being slightly puzzled. Possibly he was wanting a new game, something a bit more interesting, but he kept going. It was a good game, he did like it, and he could sense that Joe liked it too. For Joe, nothing could equal the buzz of being behind a dog on track, the cord tense, the dog pushing himself forward into his task, but then Joe knew how it could end up when done for real, when the hidden treasure wasn't a tatty bit of old rag but a criminal, or a vital piece of evidence, or a wounded victim, dying or dead in the forest.

They didn't train in buried-body searches and never would be told the real secrets, presumably in case they let slip any burying tips while chatting to potential murderers in the public bar. That was a specialist course for a very few select dogs that did nothing else. The body dog instructor would wander the lanes with a spade and a sack with a dead piglet in it, and there were pigs already underground in various spots around the fields, at different depths and of different vintages. Some had been there many years. The instructor would go to a certain place with a stick, poke it into the soil in a certain way to release the scent – to let it breathe, he would say – and the dog would have to find it. It was rumoured that some of the pigs weren't pigs at all, that a senior officer of long ago had managed to get hold of some bits of the real thing from the morgue, but that was just rumour.

The whole body dog scheme had its roots in the Brady and Hindley moors murders, when a large group of general-purpose dogs – there being no specialised body dogs at that time – had been let loose in a futile attempt to find buried children on the barren lands of Saddleworth. The result was mayhem among the dogs. Some fought, some charged about trying to work out what the new game was, some tried to bite the CID. After that, it was decided that a training course should be devised, and very good it was too. British police body dogs went to overseas wars to help find dead soldiers. In some cultures, the spirit cannot rest until the body is buried by the family, not an idea that had occurred when the training started, but one that did bring in proof that the training worked, as well as funds to help it continue. Dogs like Cass were too useful in general police work to spend the time on such a narrow specialisation and, in any case, the real experts were collies and Labradors; the latter seemed to have a particular nose for it and could have saved Mr Carter a lot of bother finding Tutankhamun.

After the last couple of tracks, Joe had taken the harness off as soon as the dog found the trophy. Harness was only worn for tracking; putting it on had to become a signal, a trigger that tracking was the next thing and all that mattered. Now Biro shuffled along to mark out the next challenge, putting a right-angled turn in the track, still in full view.

With the dog on the lead and the other students watching intently, Joe walked to a spot about five yards from the start of Biro's scuffling. 'Steady,' he said, and, 'Good lad, good boy, steady' as he put on the harness again. Cass sat, tongue out slightly, breath coming quickly, raring to go. Joe walked back a few paces, paying out the cord, and said, 'Seek.'

The dog more or less understood what 'Seek' meant. He knew it was an instruction to do something, and the something he'd been doing was finding a track. He cast about. Joe held the cord high. It was so important not to check the dog in these early stages. He mustn't stop, or jerk the cord, or allow it to tangle in the dog's legs.

'Good boy, Cass,' said Joe, quietly, as the dog knocked the start of the track and set off. Joe set off too, at a very fast walking pace, winding cord in until he was four yards or so behind the dog. In his eagerness, Cass ran straight on and overshot the right-hand, right-angle turn, as Joe and Biro fully expected him to do, and it took the dog a while to realise it. According to his experience, tracks came to an end with a rag. Here was no rag and no scent. He stopped, unable to solve the problem.

'Seek,' said Joe, and off he went again, searching in circles, always clockwise, Joe had noticed. The man stood, cord held high above his head, turning on the spot, while Cass went around him, filtering the air through a million nerve-ending sensors until the bell rang. He found the track about three-quarters of the way along, where he'd already been, on the first leg. Joe, Biro and the rest held their breath as the dog stood square on to the track, sniffing, and let their breath go in a corporate small sigh of relief when Cass turned right and followed to the point where he'd lost it, rather than turning left and backtracking.

Of course, he lost it again, but this time he needed no instructions. Two small clockwise circles and he'd knocked the second leg. Joe wound in the cord and resumed his half-trot, keeping up. This was such an important lesson to learn. Fleeing ne'er-do-wells did tend to run in straight lines, but things got in the way, ideas occurred, and the dog had to realise that losing a track did not mean the end had been reached.

Lunch was usually sandwiches in the locker room. There was a canteen over in the HQ building, but you had to dress reasonably smartly for it. Dog handlers tended to be too scruffy to bother except for the fish and chips on Fridays. In the cosiness of the locker room people could talk, read the papers, do the crossword, unless one was called into the instructors' room. There the food was a little better. Rather than being police official issue, it was bought and delivered according to an obscure arrangement with the sandwich bar around the corner.

The official card game was nomination whist. A novice, volunteered by the other students, might think he was being honoured by the instructors' invitation but he was there to be fleeced and to make up the numbers because the instructors were one short for a four. Nomination whist was basically the same as any other kind of whist except the players had to forecast the number of tricks they would take. Also known as Oh Hell, German Bridge, Blackout and Whistabix, the number of cards per hand reduced round by round and the players took turns to lead, meaning be the first to nominate and lay a card. Trumps also rotated, including 'no trumps', and the fourth player to nominate could not say a number that made the total of tricks bid equal to the number of cards dealt per hand.

The normal rate was five pence a point, going up to ten or even twenty if there was a novice handler in there. A correct forecast was worth ten points, plus one for each trick, so in theory there could always be three players correct at every hand, with everyone paying each other the difference between their scores. The students didn't know what happened when the instructors were at full strength and didn't need a sub. They just knew that when one of them went in, the theory was always proved in practice. Three players were always correct.

The whole of the first phase of training, near enough the five weeks that Joe and Cass had missed, was to do with obedience and finding. Cass would have to show that he was completely under Joe's control, from simple things like walking patiently to more difficult exercises like the long down, where Cass would have to lie still for ten minutes while Joe walked away out of sight. As well as staying put, Cass would also have to be willing on command to take on feats of athleticism: to clear the long jump at 12 feet and the 3-foot hurdle, and to get over, not necessarily to clear, the high jump at 6 feet.

Heelwork was the foundation of obedience; the girl at the gun-dog kennels had made a very good start on that. Cass sat in front of Joe, on the lead. Joe took a step forward to his left, passed the lead behind his back from right to left hand, and said, 'Heel.' Cass just did it, and sat straight and parallel, not with his backside at an angle. Joe stepped back and they did it again. Perfect. Well, that was one strand of training that had caught up the missing weeks without any bother at all. Now for the military two-step.

Joe never would get Cass to march and wheel with quite the precision that girl had managed, but he never stopped trying. As the instructor shouted left turn, right, about turn, Joe and Cass, on the lead, strode the parade ground at a brisk pace, then at the double, then at a funeral march. It looked good. Cass also knew what 'sit', 'down' and 'stand' meant. What a trainer that girl was. So Biro suggested they try it off the lead.

Cass thought this was the signal for playtime, ran across the yard to the nearest kennel and barked for fun at the surprised inmate – a small, rather refined cocker spaniel bitch that could smell heroin at a hundred paces but had no notion of how to deal with hairy ruffians like Cassius.

'Cassius, come, come, come,' shouted Joe and, reluctantly, Cass did. The lead went back on and they did it all again. There was a danger here. It was quite possible to bore a dog out of his good behaviour. No matter how much praise was given, life had to offer new and more difficult games, or at least bring around the favourite ones more often. Marching up and down was all very well, and Cass did it as required while his heart and true talents were elsewhere: in the tracking and searching he had already experienced and, if he but knew it, in games not yet played to do with finding, cornering and dominating.

Cass may sometimes have had a different opinion, but the police officer's complete control of the dog is the *sine qua non*. The dog must set off only when told to, must speak when something is found, must come when called and must let go immediately on command of whatever is in his mouth, whether it's a ball, a clue or a criminal's leg. Heelwork and simple obedience were essential and had to be kept up to the gold standard. Joe would overcome the dog's tendency to be blasé about it by springing a little heelwork on him when he wasn't expecting it. At any time, on duty or off it, Joe would give Cass an impromptu examination in Basic Police Dog – 'heel', 'sit', 'down' – and if he did it well, which he almost always did, the more amusing game of retrieve would follow.

The perfect retrieve has five steps to it. Step one: dog sits quietly by officer's left side while officer throws object. Two: on command, dog runs, picks up object and returns smartly with it. Three: dog sits in front of officer with object in mouth. Four: on command, dog allows officer to take object. Five: on command, dog walks past officer on his right hand, around the back of his legs, and sits at his left side, in line. Step five is added later, when steps one to four are fully embedded.

They removed to one of the fields to try it. The girl at the kennels had done this too. Joe had seen it, with the decoy duck or whatever it was. Cass should be straight into the routine, no problem.

Joe had a new dumb-bell, traditional pattern, being a piece of broom handle about six inches long with a wooden cube at each end. He'd not had time to modify it against the chewing he knew it was going to get, by whipping strong twine around the centre and fixing flattened pieces of baked-bean tin to the cubes to make those parts less attractive to pick up. Dogs don't like the feel of metal on their teeth any more than humans do.

Step one was fine the first time Cass did it, although he needed several extra sitting orders to keep him still while Joe, carefully holding the dumb-bell only in the middle, with finger and thumb moistened in spit, threw it not too far away. On the word 'Fetch', Cass set off at top speed, picked up the dumb-bell, tossed it in the air, picked it up again by one end, ran 20 yards further on, lay down and set about eating his prize. What dog doesn't like a stick to gnaw on?

Biro put himself on the other side of the dog, so Cass was between him and Joe, and started shouting, angrily, furiously, with venom. The dog stopped chewing and stared. There could be no mistake in Cass's mind. While he didn't know what he'd done wrong exactly, he knew that it was very wrong indeed, and this horrible man was being thoroughly nasty about it. Looking away from the angry man, Cass could see Joe, walking backwards, arms out, calling, 'Cass, come, come, come' in pleasant, welcoming tones.

Cass ran, away from the nasty instructor, to be greeted with praise and ear-rubbing and all sorts of fuss by the good guy, his friend Joe. So, they would do it again. Biro brought the dumb-bell back; Cass looked the other way.

It was not unknown for a dog to get the idea of a correct retrieve on its second or third attempt. Equally, all the instructors could tell stories about dogs that took ten, a dozen, twenty tries, and the very occasional one that never got it. Cass would be one of the former sort.

Joe sat him down and held the dumb-bell for the dog to see. Cass looked at it, looked at Joe, looked at the dumb-bell again, watched it curve through the air and land about ten yards away, and sat perfectly still. Joe felt his pleasure and confidence rise. 'Fetch,' he said, quietly and, under his breath, 'remember what that girl at the kennels taught you.' Cass picked the dumb-bell up by its middle and began trotting back, tail wagging. 'Come,' said Joe, unnecessarily, but keeping all the elements of the routine. At a slight upward nod from Joe, Cass sat, very pleased with himself. 'Leave,' said Joe. Cass let him take the dumb-bell and looked at his lord, friend and master expectantly. He'd won that game and deserved all the praise and ruffling of his great mane. Later, 'heel' would be added to the sequence, and Cass would automatically walk behind and sit after the leave, without a command. Marvellous dog.

They did the retrieve a few more times and found Cass had a habit of dropping the dumb-bell at Joe's feet instead of sitting and waiting for the leave, which was perhaps a throwback to his short but effective gun-dog training. Joe's response to a drop was to step back and say, 'Fetch', and again and again if the dog kept dropping. Cass knew very well that the game was not complete until he did the leave and the heel, but he couldn't help this small fault that had become semi-automatic and would stay with him after the training course was over. Joe would eventually cure him by using his check chain instead of the dumb-bell. Cass hated the metal in his mouth and dropped it straight away. 'Fetch', and he had to pick it up again. If he still dropped it, there were more fetches until he realised that the quickest way to get rid of the metal in his mouth was to do the sit-and-leave.

Problem solved. The dumb-bell was never dropped again, nor the other favourite toy: a police uniform trouser leg with a big knot tied in the end so it could be thrown. Joe and Cass could have a hugely enjoyable game of tuggy with this, Cass digging his paws into the ground and pulling like fury, whereupon the injustice of life would be demonstrated. The dog had the trouser leg. He deserved the trouser leg. He had won the trouser leg in combat because, after a suitable interval of game playing, he had wrested the trouser leg from his friend Joe and started ripping it to shreds. Just as he was really enjoying that, his alleged friend would say, 'Leave' and he'd have to let go. Unfair, or what?

Now that Cass had mastered the retrieve, all he had to do was adapt to operational circumstances where the object to be found and retrieved and brought to Joe was not thrown by Joe, in sight, but was already lying somewhere, possibly hidden. And, it could be anything at all, except that it would never be a home-made wooden dumb-bell or a police trouser leg with a knot in it.

Tracking would progress through older scents, up to tracks laid an hour before. Most days there would be a breeze, slight, or strong, to blow the scent off line. Unless the track happened to have been laid in perfect alignment with the wind, and the wind had not veered but had stayed exactly where it was, the dog would always be working a little or a lot downwind of the actual track as laid. So, if the track was east to west and the wind was from the south, the dog would be running some inches north of the line. Sometimes this made the handler believe the dog was making a mistake and he'd try to correct it, when somebody like Biro, if there was anyone like Biro, would shout, 'No. Watch your dog. Trust him. He's right and you're wrong. Don't try and do his thinking for him.'

Angles and turns in the track would eventually develop into the ultimate Biro test: the six-pointed star laid out of sight, which he only put down if he knew there was a dog on the course able to do it. Before that, there was the track box. Biro had laid the outfield track 20 minutes before, starting from the box. Looking from above, if Joe could have seen it, it was like the lines joining stars in a new constellation. At five yards from the nearest pole, Joe sat Cass down and kitted him up in his harness and tracking cord. The poles were not really relevant as markers for the dog. They showed the humans where the track was and neither human nor dog knew where the going-away track would start. They set off clockwise around the box with a 'seek'. The worst thing would be to go right around the box without 'finding'. Cass, nose to the ground, halfway along the second side, turned his head. This was it. 'Good boy, good boy,' said Joe, and they were off. The wind was gusting this way and that, blowing the scent about but Cass found the turn on to the second stage without bother.. The third leg's scent had been blown awry by the same wind, and when Cass did his small clockwise circles, he was out of place to hit it. All he could get was the end of the leg he'd just been along. He could have backtracked to find the corner but he didn't, and never would. He stood, considering maybe that the job was done, as it had been before, except there was no rag, of course.

'Seek, good boy,' said Joe, and off went the dog again, circling wider this time, and finding at last, and rattling along to the next corner and, glory be to God in the highest, not overshooting but turning, and Joe's heart lifted and Biro shouted, 'Yes' and Cass was home. Tracking, apparently, was a game he would be able to play at the top level; he was native to it. Joe hitched him to a fence post while the others took their turns.

Next stage would be small objects placed along the track, matchbox-sized at first but soon getting smaller. For novice handlers, the articles were pound coins, provided by the handler. He had to be able to get his learner dog back on track, so he had to know exactly where the track was. Losing pound coins concentrated the mind, so the man would definitely make it his business to know where they were and would want to be sure of his dog before moving on to pound coins blind, the sudden finding of which could look certain to cause physical injury. When the dog 'knocked' – scented – an article, his head would snap around to the side, his body would follow, and he'd finish standing at right angles to the track, scenting the article. If it was a still day he'd have been belting along right over the track and his momentum would carry him a foot or even a yard beyond the article before the message from his nose reached his brain. In a frantic attempt to correct his position and get that most sensitive and informative of sensory organs right over the object, his nose would stop and his head would duck while his body kept going. He could do a sudden, somersault-style body flip that any breakdancer would have been proud of.

Having knocked, he would want to pick up the object, to

retrieve it as he had been taught, but this training was for operational circumstances where a retrieve was not the desired outcome, so the handler would say, 'Down'. The dog by now knew what 'down' meant, but at first he would not want to do it. After fifty, seventy-five or a hundred times of finding the article, the dog would go down without his handler saying anything.

As well as the track box there was the property square, 25 yards by 25 yards, also marked by four poles in the ground, which was meant to represent any enclosed space such as a garden, with small objects placed inside the imaginary boundaries for the dog to find. All the grass in the square would have been trampled flat so there were no tracks to follow. When the dogs were learning to find, the objects were the size of the legendary matchbox. Eventually, thought Joe, getting ambitious, if Cass was to become a real expert, he'd be able to find things smaller than a pound coin: a one-inch piece of bootlace perhaps, a half or even a quarter of a .22-cartridge case.

In fact, as an exercise property square was rather oriented towards shows and trials and had not been devised purely for practical, dog-handling reasons. Except for the odd occasion – Cass would have one at a burglary when it was believed nothing had been stolen – the nearest equivalent operationally would have been walking down a road and searching the verge. Even then, with concerns over DNA, you would want your dog to find but not pick up, whereas property square was about finding and retrieving.

The dog would never understand that he was to search only inside an invisible square marked by four red-and-white poles and, to start with, he would not want to search it at all but to stick close to his handler, who was not permitted to cross the imaginary lines. One day in the future, Joe would click his fingers and point, and Cass would go search where indicated or, if the dog was in the wrong place altogether, Joe would clap his hands, point and say, 'Find.'

Meanwhile, he would stay as close to Cass as he could, moving with the direction of the search, and would never allow the dog to feel that his master's attention was wandering. Joe had to watch Cass closely anyway, as his indication of a find, of winding the object, might be the merest twitch of the head. Joe would then say nothing, but move to the nearest point on the invisible line so that when Cass picked up the coin, or whatever it was, he had the shortest possible distance to go and so the least opportunity to drop it. If he did drop it, it had to be found all over again.

The objective, the test of competence, was to search the whole square and to find and retrieve three articles in five minutes. Trying the exercise for the first time, Cass sat beside Joe, about three yards outside the invisible line on the downwind side of the square. The three yards was a measure with a purpose. When the dog set off, he would have moved about three yards by the time he got his nose down to search, so he'd be just inside the square to begin.

Cass sat peaceably at first, but soon tensed as he watched the instructor toss a small object (a plastic brick from a toddler's building set) from hand to hand. Joe felt Cass strain. He wanted to have a go at this new game. 'Sit,' said Joe, quietly. The instructor tossed the brick a few more times, put it down and stepped back out of the way. Joe said, 'Find' and slipped the lead. 'Find' was the command for property, 'seek' the instruction for tracking. Cass would soon learn the difference.

Half a second before Cass picked the brick up, Joe was running backwards, shouting 'Come, come, come', and Cass ran back with the brick in his mouth. 'Leave.' He looked at Joe's outstretched hand with mild curiosity. 'Leave.' More mild curiosity, plus a slight crunching of the plastic. 'Cassius. Leave!' Oh, all right, I didn't want your rotten brick anyway.

Progression in the property square was a gradual thing, taking most of the course. The next stage would be three articles put down showily by the instructor so the dog could see them, then three articles put down secretly but so the handler knew where they were, then smaller and smaller articles put down blind.

By this time, dogs and handlers had reached various standards, from 'almost always reliable' to 'generally does OK considering'. Even the best were not perfect. Nobody was perfect, not even Cass.

That night there was a trip arranged to a pub in the neighbouring force's main city, about fifty miles away. One of the lads had phoned a friend and asked him which of the pubs on his manor (a) kept the best pint and (b) had a landlady who thought sawdust on the floor an unnecessary luxury.

'Has it got to be a landlady?' said the mate.

'Definitely,' said the trip arranger. 'We don't want to get into any fights.'

'In which case, you want the Knob and Knocker.'

'There is no pub called the Knob and Knocker.'

'Its real name is the Dog and Partridge, but you can get anything there. Anything at all.'

And so it was that six happy policemen, including a revitalised Joe Sleightholm, boarded a minibus for the bright lights. 'Where we going?' asked Joe.

'Mystery tour,' said Dave Archer. 'Glen arranged it. I think it's a 1920s Russian film at the New Arts Cinema, silent with subtitles, followed by tea and biscuits and a discussion group.'

The talk in the bus was of dogs to start with, and stories from their pre-dog days. Joe told one about the time he was in a village shop, chatting to the owner about some kids who'd been trying to nick sweets, when a woman came up to him and said, 'It's a crying shame. And what are you going to do about it?'

'I'm going to see the parents and have a quiet word,' said Joe.

'Not those bleeding kids,' said the woman. 'They want a good hiding. No, I mean the squatters. The squatters at Mrs Bradshaw's.' It turned out that Mrs Bradshaw, a disabled and elderly lady, had been invaded by a group of, as the woman put it, long-haired druggy scrotes on the social, and her life was being made a misery. Joe took the address and went round there.

'What did you do, Joe?' said Dave. 'Kick the bastards out?'

'Certainly not,' said Joe. 'You know that sort of thing isn't allowed. No, no. As my report stated, I gained entrance through a window that had been broken, possibly by a stone thrown up from a passing car. Then I attended while the squatters left at the lady's request.'

'I was on nights once, on the beat, and I happened to meet a dog handler,' said Glen. 'Left the force now, but I think that's when I first got the idea. Anyway, we were chatting, standing at the top of this hill, about midnight, keeping an eye on a hotel car park, which was full of classic cars. There was a classic-car auction on next day at the hotel. We saw this lad – well, young man really – obviously pissed as a fart, reeling around this car park, heading in our direction. What he was doing was unscrewing the chromium petrol caps, you remember them, off some of the cars that happened to take his fancy. So I arrested him and took him off to the station and left the dog handler to keep watch.'

'Is that it?' said Dave. 'What kind of a story is that?'

'I haven't finished yet, Constable Archer, if you would be so kind. This lad was an artist. He specialised in light-reflecting sculptures, which are those things that seem to move although they're not moving, and he'd been struck with the idea of making one out of the petrol caps. Well, we were in court, and I didn't want to be hard on the lad so I told the truth. *Your worships, we observed the defendant removing the petrol caps, and challenged him. Whereupon the defendant replied, "Nice doggy."* True, that. And I kept a straight face.'

The bus had reached the ring road. As they turned towards the centre they saw the estates of tower blocks, and as they turned off the main road to wind their way through the back streets of the dirty old part of the city, where the sun refused to shine, they began speculating on the potential for dog work. Every street corner had young lads lounging at it. Shops that were closed were metal shuttered. Shops that were open either sold cigarettes and booze or some kind of fast food. They were all over the place, take-aways of every kind, showing the high incidence in the district of families where a parent would rather give the kids a couple of quid to buy a kebab than cook a meal for them.

There were plenty of lock-ups where necessary engineering and cosmetic operations could be performed on cars that were missing their paperwork, and plenty of dark alleys convenient for business transactions featuring herbal extracts. They even passed along a street behind a factory that had lamp-posts at regular intervals and young ladies in short skirts leaning on them.

'It's Ealing Studios,' said one.

'No,' said another, 'it's *Doctor Who*. We're going to meet Doctor Who and he's going to take us to a planet far away, where the bobbies all have flowers in their hair.'

The bobbies in the bus tried to imagine what would happen if all six of them turned up one night with their dogs and did a sweep right through this locality. They joked about it but they all had that feeling, that nervous excitement, let's-go-get-'em mixed with memories of colleagues being stabbed and hit with bricks, of dogs being walloped with baseball bats, of coppers and dogs being shot, plus the professional knowledge, gained through experience, that the uniform is no protection in that world they were seeing through the windows of their little bus.

The Dog and Partridge was about as far away from sporting country as it was possible to be, but at least it was in a street of houses, stone-built Victorian houses, rather than being the oasis in a desert of high rises. Two doors down from it was an inviting establishment calling itself Kee Hong and proclaiming the availability of finest Pekinese and Cantonese cuisine. Joe was sent to negotiate a constabulary table d'hôte price for chicken chow mein, barbecued spare ribs, house special curry and special fried rice, all times six, while the rest decided to enter the pub one by one, knowing that whoever was in there would be able to recognise an off-duty police officer from ten miles away.

The first one in had the required reaction: silence, followed by grumbles with a threatening undertone. There was no one behind the bar. He walked up to it, turned his back on it, elbows resting and beamed as he surveyed the scene, stopping short of saying good evening. The next man came in.

'Hello, Dave,' said the first, in mock surprise. 'What are you on?'

'Nights,' said Dave. 'Oh, you mean… pint of bitter, please, Glen.'

The landlady appeared as number three walked in. 'Gentlemen. What can I get you? Are you hoping to meet anyone in particular?'

The fourth came in as Glen spoke. 'Six pints of bitter, please. Timothy Taylor. The others'll be here in a minute. No, we're not meeting anyone. Just half a dozen working blokes out on the town. On our day off.'

CHAPTER FOUR

LOVE ME, LOVE MY DOG

Julia had been a waitress in a quite genteel café when Joe first saw her. He'd called at the café, on Clufford High Street, making door-to-door enquiries about a team of shoplifters he wanted to trace, and there was this petite brunette, quite a lot younger than him and a great deal shorter, with a brilliant smile and a lilt in her walk that were more than enough to make Joe forget about the shoplifters.

Julia was used to making a hit with men and thought no more of this tall, slightly hesitant policeman. The last thing she wanted in her life was another suitor; previously ditched boyfriends never seemed to give up and in any case her sights were adjusted for more golden targets than a common copper. The current beau was a young gentleman beneficiary of the sale, many years before, of his family's chain of chemist's shops to Boots. He liked to drive his Alvis three-litre drophead coupé over the hills to Sutton Bank where he was a member of the gliding club, and Julia liked to go with him although she refused to go up in a glider. This young man's idea of hard work was trying to work out whether Farewell My Lovely at eleven to two was a better bet than Zambomba at thirteen to eight, but never mind. He had good manners.

Then that very tall policeman started coming into the café for his breakfast, or for tea and cake depending on his shift, not in his uniform of course, just in casual clothes. He did walk past sometimes in his uniform, giving a glance through the window, and even came in once with some story about a rascally type with a ginger beard and a Scottish accent trying to pass forged notes of the Bank of Brigadoon. He came again, this time asking Julia to keep an eye out for a group of nuns in sunglasses, because yesterday they'd run from a Chinese restaurant without paying and, the day before, tricked the man with the hot dog van out of six frankfurters with onions and mustard. It was only when he arrived looking very concerned, to warn Julia about anyone trying to sell stock from a hijacked lorry-load of hundreds and thousands, silver dragées and chocolate vermicelli that she clicked.

Many laughs and a whirlwind romance later, Julia had discarded all thoughts of a thick, boring and wealthy husband and settled instead for fun and a policeman's wage. Naturally, she assumed that she'd soon be an inspector's wife, or even a detective superintendent's.

Julia was only 27 weeks into her first pregnancy when the waters broke, or rather, not so much broke as sprung a leak. The doctor came and immediately summoned an ambulance into which she was loaded with great care and driven to the hospital as if she were made of spun sugar. The leak kind of dried up, but they kept her in for observation.

Julia and Joe had been decorating the boxroom to establish it as the nursery for their first child, which made it necessary to decorate their own room and the guest bedroom, with the result that Painter Joe was currently sleeping on a Li-Lo in the designated nursery. He awoke at about three in the morning in what he imagined was an air raid. Searchlights swept the sky. There were bangs and booms. Dimly through the confusion of an enemy attack on his house in a north country village, he heard his name.

There was a man knocking on his bedroom window, shining a torch on his ceiling and shouting for him. 'Joe. Joe. It's us. It's the fuzz. Wake up, you stupid sod.'

At the door he met two police constables. He knew the senior one, who explained that they'd phoned and phoned, then climbed up to the front bedroom, had no reply and so woken the next-door neighbour to ask if Joe was dead or had been seen. Although the bobby's initial assumption as to which was Joe and Julia's normal bedroom had been correct, he wasn't as up to date as the neighbour who had explained that they were painting it. Try the little one at the back, had been his advice, a room too far to hear the phone. So the senior constable sent the junior one up the ladder to shine his light through the curtainless window and fetch Joe down to hear the news. Which was?

'Your wife's had a baby,' said the constable. 'You've got to get there quick. Car all right?'

It was all right, all right. Joe was dressed, in it and gone in a single moment and, 11 miles or three seconds later, was walking, or rather flapping hysterically, down the corridor of the hospital's maternity unit. The night sister picked him out. She was small and handsome, a trim person, with that special night-sisterly blend of charm, concern, compassion and don't-mess-with-me-brother.

'Mr Sleightholm?'

'Mmmmodddiffwwassgabli?'

'It's a little girl.'

If he'd had more presence of mind, perhaps he might have said, 'I bet it is. Little, I mean.'

'Do you smoke, Mr Sleightholm?' said the sister.

'No, actually. I gave up a few weeks ago.'

'Well,' she said, dipping into her dark-blue breast pocket behind a pinny as crisp and white as a choir-boy's collar, bringing out a scrunched-up packet of Old Holborn and some green Rizlas. 'I think you'd better start again. I'll call you when you can see them.'

He sat outside in the night air and tried to keep some of the threads of tobacco inside the paper, drawing on student's rolling skills, which did not include how to stop a sudden surge of St Vitus' dance. A nurse came to tell him that his wife was being kept quiet for the moment with gentle sedation and he couldn't see the baby yet.

It appeared that Julia had gone to the lavatory at about 2am but quickly became convinced that she was in the wrong place. Bells had been rung, medics had dashed about, something approximating to a baby had been from its mother's womb untimely ripped. Mother was in a state of shock, semiconsciousness and terrified foreboding but otherwise was well, whereas baby was 1 lb and 14 oz, or 850 g.

Eventually, Joe was taken to look. Through a glass screen he saw a doctor, younger than him, white coat, face of adamant concentration, elbows up and hands on a tangle of needles, fine wires, thin pipes and more needles. He looked like a man looks when he knows how to carve a duck but can't quite remember what he did last time. The focus of his attention and now Joe's, was a transparent-skinned, alien life form – a cross between ET, a nonagenarian woman and a raw pork sausage. It was indeed very little. A pint pot would have been several sizes too big for it. He could see the bones in its minuscule hands. It – she – could have put both her hands inside a snowdrop.

The doctor saw Joe and shook his head furiously. Father was not welcome at this stage: he was a distraction, an intruding spectator, when the life form had to be connected by means of needles and tubes to machines, bottles, bags, all manner of magic. There didn't seem to be enough room on the life form's surface for so many needles. In any case, what miniature blood vessels were there, beneath said surface, that were of sufficient diameter to take a needle? He went and sat beside his sleeping wife in a dazed state.

The odds, they were told, were eight to one against. One out of every nine very premature babies survived. In their favour was the sex. She was a girl and girls were much better at it than boys. Against that was the fact that she was the youngest, the most premature survivor, they had ever had to deal with in that hospital.

They put her in a clear plastic box with a lid, like a garden propagator. She didn't take up much space in it, not even with all her needles and tubes, she being hardly more than six or seven inches long – sixteen centimetres or so. Joe went home, made daily visits and, a couple of weeks later, Julia came home. They settled into a routine. Every day they drove to the hospital to look at the baby in the propagator. They sat beside her and watched her wrestle with death. Then they went home.

They came to dread the telephone. The nurses rang regularly to say that the baby, now called Holly, had had a heart attack, or she'd recovered from a bad night, or she was stable, or less stable, or she might not get through the weekend, or she had pneumonia. When that phone rang, they felt pure fear.

After a few weeks, Holly was improving and considered well enough to move into a new kind of box: one without a lid. The intensive care unit had a room with these boxes around the walls. On Joe and Julia's right as they went in were the boxes with babies connected to the beeping machines and the bags. As a new baby arrived, everybody moved around one and, when you got all the way round and were last on the left, you'd be beepless and bagless and you'd just about made it.

Every day, without exception it seemed, as they went to look into their box there was a box empty nearby that had been occupied yesterday. Those parents had come like Joe and Julia to look into their box, at their little battler, and had taken their grief home and would come no more, while Holly's box kept moving round the room. Still there were alarms. Still the phone rang but, gradually, the tension eased. The nurses put her photograph on the noticeboard: good sign. Holly was going to be a one-in-niner.

After three months, more or less on the day she should have been born, they came to the hospital to take their baby home. They knew all the nurses by name and there were tears as well as beams and hugs. Joe had heard that when they were on nights the nurses liked a glass of sherry. He confirmed this with a little detective work, sneaking into the chaotic area they called both office and rest room and looking in a few cupboards and so, rather than a donation to be swallowed up in hospital funds, he made a pathetic attempt to thank the wonderful, dedicated, supremely skilled, lovely nurses and doctors with a dozen bottles of as good an amontillado as he could possibly afford.

Holly now weighed a little over five pounds, or two and a bit kilos. Joe and Julia were bemused. To them, babies were things you went to visit in a hospital, but here she was, on the back seat of the car, in a carrycot. They didn't dare go straight home with this strange creature, so they went to the pub. The landlord had a look and said, 'Hello. I'm your Uncle Frank.'

Since then, Joe and Julia had had another daughter, Harriet, also premature but by nothing like so much, and the family had grown up a little. Now it was time for Julia to meet Cassius. Holly (aged seven) and Harriet (aged three) would need to feel safe with the dog, and be fond of him, so Joe had to know exactly what Cass would do.

Joe and Cass had had four weeks together, Cass staying at the school for the weekends with Joe popping in to see him, feed and water him and keep the ties binding. The next small step in their relationship was to introduce him to his new permanent home, the kennel in Joe's garden previously occupied by Joe's other police dog, and to his new permanent family, which included the family pet GSD, the matronly, mature and superior bitch Leila.

Cass's new home was made from half a dozen flagstones, some sand and cement, a flatpack kennel and various pieces of wire mesh and steel rod. Joe had laid the stones, installed the flatpack, bolted the metal together and there was the run, two by three yards and two yards high. Sleeping quarters were one, by one-and-a-half, by one. Leila the family pet had exactly the same, police issue, but on the other side of the garden.

Young Cass may not have met such an older bitch before and almost certainly not one of the calibre of the Lady Leila. Like most of his kind, Cass would not be aggressive towards a female and may even defer to one, and would be reluctant to attack a female human too, no matter what offences she had committed or what dangers she presented. Of course, this gentlemanly attitude did not work the other way and the first thing Leila did on meeting Cass was to bite him on his ear. It wasn't a hard bite; more of a nip really, a status nip, telling Cass that while he was welcome, cautiously welcome, at Castle Sleightholm, he had better remember that he was a mere pageboy, a knave of the lower orders, here by the permission, graciously granted, of She Who Must Be Obeyed.

Cass accepted his place in the hierarchy and seemed happy enough to be put in his kennel with his dinner and an old sweater of Joe's for atmosphere. Julia came out to look and, seeing her as a threat to his food, Cass gave her a growl and a fairly apologetic bark. Julia laughed at him, called him a few light-hearted names and said she thought he was rather handsome, actually.

Joe had a little plan for his evening, pre-dinner walk with Cass, so he sloped off to the woods down the back lane to lay a track. This was something he would do throughout his time with Cass, on duty or off, whatever the weather. If tracking was to become second nature in Cass, he needed constant practice to keep his skills sharp. A year on from now, Joe would set long tracks with tight corners and twisty turns and leave them for three or four hours before coming back. At the end of the track would be Cass's ball or his current toy of preference. These would be done in harness. Free practice tracks were generally more realistic, in a straight or simply curving line, maybe only half an hour old.

Today, at the earliest stages of his development, Cass would be asked to follow a half-hour straight track in harness. He would know he'd achieved success in his task when he found, at the end of the track, his most prized possession: a model of King Kong made of hard rubber. Always on the lookout for such things – a plentiful and continual supply being necessary – Joe had picked it out of a skip.

Joe and Julia would eat later, so while she fed the kids, Joe took Cass out. There were footpaths, fields and woods all around, and farmers, naturally. Joe started Cass on his track, went through a gate and was appalled to see that one of these farmers, getting his last job in before dark, had spread slurry over Joe's footprints. Cass, straining on his long lead and leaning into his harness, still wanted to go and so Joe, no wellies, had to follow.

Cass was not in the remotest bit upset by the slurry. He followed Joe's smell through this extraneous layer of liquid cow muck as if it wasn't there. Joe was astonished. Later, talking to Biro about it, he would be told that it was perfectly normal behaviour for a good tracker and nothing to shout about, but at the time Joe was thrilled to the core. Just as Cass paid no attention to the covering layer of bovine waste, so Joe in his pleasure couldn't care less about the same substance soaking into his new canvas loafers. They would wash, and so would Cass's feet when he'd found his toy, had a tuggy with it, and walked with Joe down to the little stream that flowed through the wood.

At least, that was the plan, but Cass could not see that his feet needed washing, or, more truthfully, he couldn't see that he needed to stand in that water. He didn't like water. Standing in water made him unhappy. Joe thought Cass was being silly and, jumping over the stream back and forth, called Cass to him each time, so the dog had to get his feet wet. Stupid animal. What a nancy. Call yourself a police dog?

Next morning, Sunday, Joe took his two girls to see Cassius, the new teddy bear. He was pleased to see Joe, as always, but took no notice of the children. It would take a few weekends before Joe would let the girls stroke Cass, but for now he was quite sure he could let the dog out, get Holly to throw a ball for him, and generally let everyone get used to each other. Harriet was a bit scared of this beast that was so much bigger than she was, but there was no problem.

Neither was there a problem when they went for a short family walk that afternoon. So as not to complicate matters, they left Leila at home. Cass walked tidily on Joe's left side for twenty minutes or so, until little Harriet began to complain. 'Are we nearly there yet?'

Joe gave the dog lead to Julia and took Harriet up on his shoulders as they turned for home. Cass, seeing his master otherwise occupied in an important task, snapped in close to Julia and walked with her in proper, close-up disciplined fashion. Had it been a rainy day, Julia's jeans would have been every bit as wet and muddy as Joe's often were. As they came in sight of home, with Julia in front, Cass on her left and Holly on her right hand, Joe felt that mixture of emotions which brings a certain tightness to the throat and which is usually followed by a tear. Well, it was nothing to be ashamed of. He had a lovely family and the best job in the world.

* * * * *

Cass's instinct was to protect the chosen few from the rest of the universe. Selection for membership of the few was something Cass did according to his own criteria and, at first anyway, there was always some uncertainty about that membership. It might be honorary and full for life, or just associate membership, or something in between.

As well as protecting the chosen few, Cass also protected his own property. There was always the danger, as Joe saw, that Cass could be confused if a clash arose between the two instincts. With small children around, anything could happen.

The matter was brought into the open the following Saturday when Julia was out shopping and Joe was looking after the children. Holly, walking in the garden towards the house past a dozing Cassius, noticed a clothes peg on the ground. She assumed Mummy had dropped it and so went to pick it up. Wrong. This particular clothes peg had recently become the property of Cassius. It was his peg and nobody was going to take it from him.

In a flash he stood up, growled and took Holly's arm in his mouth. He didn't bite, because it was Holly, but it was his clothes peg. Holly screamed. She thought Cass was going to eat her arm. Joe rushed out of the house, gave Cass the dressing down of his life (partly because Joe felt so guilty himself) and locked him in his run. He warned Holly and little Harriet, who was now crying because something bad had happened although she didn't quite know what, never to go near Cass's toys. Holly protested that it wasn't a toy, it was a peg, and she hated dogs because they had big teeth for biting, and she too burst into tears.

This was a problem Joe would have to do something about, and quickly. If Julia came home with the matter unresolved, an isolated incident could escalate into a global crisis. *How could the children be safe with a great huge savage dog like that running about the place? Bloody thing's bigger than the two girls put together. He will have to go, and that's it. Can't be trusted. It's your family or that dog, Joe.*

He gave the children their tea, all smiles now that memories of clothes pegs had been temporarily replaced by fish fingers and beans, and strawberry Viennetta. After tea, Joe spoke to Holly in his reasonable-father voice.

'Holly, I want you to help me feed Cass. It's his tea time too.'

'I don't want to, Daddy. I don't like Cass. He's horrible. He bit me.'

'He didn't mean to. Anyway, he didn't really bite. He was just saying it was his. What would you do, if Harriet came and pinched one of your Sylvanians?'

'She can have it. I'm too old for Sylvanian Families now.'

'Tell you what, Holly. You just come and help me put his food in his bowl. Please? For me?'

A few minutes later, Joe was walking across the lawn to Cass's run, closely followed by daughter Holly, who was carrying the dog's bowl in outstretched hands. Cass emerged from his kennel, tail wagging, looking as if butter wouldn't melt. Joe opened the little door, Holly went in with the bowl, put it down and backed out as fast as she could. Joe took her in his arms, held her high and whirled her about, at which Cass left his food to bark.

'There, you see, Holly? He's telling me not to hurt you. He's telling me to put you down or else he'll want to know why not. See? It's all about protecting. He's protecting the little one against the big one, like he'll protect his family – us – against any outsiders and people he doesn't know.'

'And his toys against everybody in the whole world.'

'That's it, Holly. You've got it. Now, we'll put Harriet in the pushchair and take Cass for a walk, hey?'

All through police training, treats in the usual sense were never used. There could be no expectations of biscuits or liver tablets on duty, but at home on Sunday morning things could be different. Joe wanted to introduce the family, including Cass, to a new game called Trust and Paid For.

'Now, first, we make Cass sit. Sit, Cass. Good boy. Now we put a biscuit down, in this case a gravy bone. Cass, sit. Sit! Good boy. Now we say, "Trust", in a long, low voice, like "Trerrrrst", OK? Julia, you say it. Good. Now Holly, you say it. Again.'

Cass sat there, bemused, looking at the gravy bone while the members of his tribe called to him in this new way. He glanced up at Joe, swished his tail and looked at the little brown biscuit again.

'Now,' said Joe, 'once you've got him settled with the gentle, low tone of your voice, you've got to pick him up. You could say, "Yippee", or "Chinese chippee", or "Third door on the left". Anything. It doesn't matter. It's the tone of voice. You've said, "Trust" in a way that means "Stay there" to Cass. Now you say, "Paid for" in a way that means "Come and get it", so you say it in a high voice with lots of excitement, like your team has scored a goal. OK? Right. All together. One, two, three: "Paid for!"'

Cass grabbed the biscuit and ran twice around the garden, stopping only to have a brief bark at Leila, snoozing in her run, and returning to sit perfectly straight in front of the family, tail swishing, clearly in expectation of further treats. They did it again and again until Cass could resist the biscuit without being told a second time to sit, but ran out of gravy bones before Holly could achieve her ambition of doing this trick with Cass on her own.

'Next week,' said Joe. 'We'll do it again next week. Just you and Cass.'

'What about Jaffa Cakes?' said Holly. 'I know we've got some. Mummy bought them yesterday. Can't we do it more now, with Jaffa Cakes?'

'No chocolate for dogs. Very, very bad for them. And now I'm going to show you how to clean his teeth.' He took a clear plastic bag from his pocket and opened it. 'See this? You know how the dentist uses that sharp curved hook thing to scrape your teeth? Well, this is the same, except it's a small electrical screwdriver, as you can see, washed in Dettol to make it super clean.'

'Are Cass's teeth electric?' asked Holly.

CHAPTER FIVE

A GREAT OBSERVER

New challenges were coming all the time for Joe and Cassius, with more variables and greater dynamics. Starting off five weeks behind the rest meant that Biro often had to spend backward-bobby time with the pair of them, although Joe pointed out that he had done the course before so it was really backward-doggy time. Part of the art of training was to keep the animal stimulated with novelty, and always to finish on success. Little, often and winning were the keys to all the exercises, including those aimed at arresting criminals: find-and-speak, with the target in the open or hidden; search for people hidden in buildings and briar patches; chase-and-stand-off, which is stopping a running suspect and detaining him by barking. Chase-and-attack, detaining by biting including armed suspects, was left until last.

Joe's confidence increased as he thought about this side of things. He had no doubts that Cass could detain, if Joe could control him, and no doubts that a pursued criminal would do almost anything rather than be attacked by Cass. And, he seemed to have a special talent for finding, although they hadn't tried it in a building yet. German Shepherds could get confused in buildings and lose their focus. Which, of course, was why spaniels and Labradors had been brought in as drug and bomb dogs. They were better at it, they stuck at it longer, a spaniel could get into places a GSD couldn't, and they didn't bite people. A dog like Cass might lose confidence in, say, a drug search and not be sure what he was supposed to do: find an unusual object or bite the man from Customs and Excise.

A light breeze in winter is the ideal for a find-and-speak in the woods. The wind blows the scent of the quarry through and around, broadcasting it, but you don't want so strong a wind that it will blow the scent right away. When The Inkspots sang 'Whispering Grass' they were right on the button: 'Don't you tell it to the breeze, 'cause she will tell the birds and bees, and everyone will know, because you told the blabbering trees.' The dog had an extra advantage in winter because the blabbering trees didn't have leaves to absorb and deflect the scent.

On this crisp and fine middle March morning, the trees were in bud and there wasn't a lot of wind but what there was blew along the length of the Ten Acre Wood. With the whole class of six dogs and six handlers watching, Biro trotted up the path waving his arms about. He had a repertoire of crazy behaviours, meant to get the dogs' blood up – Bollywood dancer, Boston Red Sox cheerleader, aerobics for the over-eighties, Mick Jagger puppet – but this was a new one with, as yet, no official name. Joe said it looked like a penguin trying to fly. Glen said it looked like Charlie Chaplin imitating a penguin trying to fly.

Biro stopped, flapped his wings a few more times, and dived off into the trees, but not far. He was still in view and it was Joe's first turn. 'Hey you, this is the police, come out or I'll send the dog,' shouted Joe, putting as much excitement into it as he could. He couldn't say, 'Come out, you stupid, half-witted, bumbling cretin; don't you realise that if you carry on doing what you're doing, you will be skewered with a scaffolding pole and barbecued on a spit for the whole of eternity?' but he had to try and convey the sentiment. The dog would be stimulated to strive harder at the game, although the precise nature of the game wasn't quite clear yet.

'Hey you, this is the police, come out or I'll send the dog,' called Joe again. The words and the manner in which they were spoken were a trigger, really addressed to the dog rather than the quarry. There was no expectation that Biro, playing the part of a criminal, would actually come out and surrender, nor would there be much expectation of that when it was done operationally. Criminals tended not to surrender, believing they had a better chance if they stayed hidden, and in any case they might not have heard what the police officer said, if he hadn't said it very loudly.

The first few runs at find-and-speak were done purely by sight, with the dog on the lead. There were always two excited 'Hey you' calls, followed by a big flourish of 'Where is he?' Cass led Joe to Biro and sat in front of him. By this time, Cass knew Biro well and looked at him with a certain amount of respect, mixed with pleasured anticipation because his appearance always signalled a game, mixed with a sideways, squinty kind of puzzlement because Biro was liable to do idiotic things. For example, at the moment, having been standing quietly next to a sycamore tree, he was practising for the annual police gurning competition, screwing his face up, sticking his tongue out and doing a hand-jive with his ears, but not moving around too much. Later on in the training course, a lot of body movement would be the trigger for chasing and biting. Encouragement to bark, not bite, was the objective here.

Cass was quite happy to watch Biro's grotesque facial contortions and after half a minute, Biro, fully prepared in case his gurning didn't work, pulled out Cass's favourite toy of the moment. Toys were never made of wood. Apart from the possibility of splinters in the mouth, it would not be a good idea to track a runaway into a wood only for the dog to come out proudly wagging his tail with a stick in his mouth. For some time, Cass's toy had been his King Kong. With only one limb left, it was literally on its last leg. Well, as soon as he saw Biro with his King Kong he went barking mad, whereupon Biro gave him the toy and reverted to normal, while Joe gave Cass lavish praise and much ear rubbing. All three of them turned and ran out of the wood, dog and handler to stand with the rest to watch the next turn. The whole class did this twice each, then it was time to progress.

The next stage was to let Cass off the lead. Joe would have to stay very close. Cass had mastered that part of the game that had him sitting and barking at the open man, but the phenomenon of the bouncing front paws had Joe a little worried in case it turned out to be more than a Cassius idiosyncrasy and rather led to a leaping attempt to rip out the throat. Biro set off, Cass strained at the lead, Joe let him go. It was too easy, and Cass made no attempt to leap on Biro. More gurning made Cass bark as Joe came up. Cass on lead, more heaps of praise, run out and watch the others.

There was still a long way to go. Training was a slow progression of two steps forward, one back, do the second one again, two more forward. Sure enough, if any criminal ever stood still behind a tree, after being given half a minute's start in sight of Cass, he would be quickly found by the dog on or off the lead and, if he made funny faces, Cass would bark. This basic behaviour had to be turned into second nature, to make the dog reliable on his own, away from his handler, in any operational circumstance. There was vocabulary to add, not so much the dog-learning words as learning tones of voice and strings of sounds that were clearly commands, usually to do with barking. It was not so difficult to set a dog like Cass off on a search or a chase. It was a natural thing to do. Keeping a prisoner in one place by barking at him in a threatening way is something a GSD can do but it needs to be taught and it needs to be commanded, sometimes from a distance. The dog wouldn't know the difference between 'Watch him', 'Scotch him' or 'Put a notch in him', but he'd learn that if his friend makes certain urgent noises charged with adrenalin and excitement he must take on the charge, get excited and bark.

Cass was not a great bystander. This was a good game and he wanted to play it, not spectate. Well, he had to behave and be civilised. Not too civilised, of course.

Next day there was more progression. Starting on the other side of the wood, so the dogs made no association between venue and game, they repeated yesterday's find-by-sight off the lead. That was good, everybody happy, all the dogs delighted, then Cass had to watch something new. Biro did his usual performance, running up the path in a guise of his choosing, then disappearing, but Solo's handler, Glen Conway, spun the dog around to disorient him. He would have to use his nose and he did it beautifully. They all did. This was the best game so far. Biro, being a big fan of Henry Cooper, always took care on find-and-speak days to splash all over an extra quantity of Brut, which led to complaints about air pollution at the lunchtime card table but did help Cass and the other dogs learn a trick or two.

Biro addressed his class. 'In the next stage, gentlemen, I shall not run away from you but rather I shall sneak into the woods and suddenly emerge, materialise or manifest myself, where the dog can see me, and do my award-winning interpretation of the Ballet Egyptien after the style of Wilson, Keppel and Betty. I shall then dematerialise into the undergrowth in a certain direction. Then, while you spin your dog, I shall move away somewhere else entirely. Behind a tree, possibly. A more portly instructor would stick out either side but I shall be invisible. When you've all cracked that one, it'll be dinner time.'

Finding Biro without knowing where to start was the point at which the whispering grass and blabbering trees came in. Cass waited impatiently outside the wood, sitting close to Joe's left side after being told to do so several times. Biro appeared and did his sand dance, singing, 'I've got a gal called Elouisa Waterbottle, she lives down in Burton on Trent', and exited stage left. He really should have been on the halls. He was a variety act in his own lunchtime.

Joe spun Cass around while Biro headed for his favourite tree, an oak in the very centre of the wood that he liked because it gave the trainee dogs a good run no matter where the wind was coming from.

'Hey you, this is the police, come out or I will send the dog,' said Joe, twice, then released the dog as promised. Cass, expecting to see Biro running away at the start of the game, could not decide which way to go and so didn't go anywhere. He was downwind, the trees were more or less bare, the brambles and last year's dead undergrowth were whispering nicely, but the rules of the game had not been followed. 'Come out or I will send the dog,' said Joe again, with feeling. 'Where is he?' Cass didn't know. Sorry, don't understand the question. 'Where is he?' said Joe, urgently, gesturing towards the wood. Cass got up, looked at Joe, and sat down again. Joe had just been telling him to sit, and most insistent he'd been about it. 'Cassius,' said Joe, more urgently still, 'come out or I'll send the dog,' and took a few steps towards the edge of the wood. Cass clicked. This was the 'finding the man behind the tree' game, but a different version.

To Cass, a waft of Biro's Brut was like a flare path to a pilot. Once he was on to it there was no way you could stop him landing. He might even have had the edge on Solo in that exercise. Joe and Glen smiled at each other as they walked back for lunch. Nothing wrong with a little rivalry.

Later in the course, when everyone was up to scratch, the

students would take turns to hide, tethering their dogs to secure fence posts while they were away. The posts had to be secure or the dogs, desperate to join in the game, would have pulled them out of the ground. Without the great waft of Brut, the smell that shouldn't be there, the signal beckoning among myriad woodland scents might not be so strident in its appeal. Even so there would be sweat, and shaving soap, and fabric softener, and bacon sandwich, and last night's pub and the post-breakfast cigarette or mint if he was giving up – plenty for a dog to go on. There would be loud and enthusiastic cries of 'Where is he?' if the dog lost concentration or got fed up, and the prey-actor would do less and less to encourage barking, eventually just standing there.

The establishment scent of a small deciduous wood is a complex matter, with many plants, animals, birds and insects contributing many different notes and chords in many keys, major and minor. An untrained human might pick up a few of the scented strands if they were close by, and another strand or two on the wind if it were a more scented season. Wild garlic and wild cherry blossom in spring, the rotting body of a fox in summer; a human, with the normal ability to distinguish between several thousand different smells, would pick up on those all right, if not on the rabbit that had passed this way a few minutes before or the woodcock sitting a few yards upwind.

The amount of a substance producing a detectable smell is so small as to be immeasurable without sophisticated scientific instruments, so put a 500-millionth of a milligram of mercaptan, a sulphurous kind of alcohol that is one of the smelliest things on earth, in half a litre of air, and a good human smeller would smell it. Cut that infinitesimal quantity into a hundred slices and put one slice in your air, and a dog would smell it easily. A human can also follow a strong scent trail and, with training, can get better at it, suggesting that uncivilised, undistracted humans who have not had their senses bombed out by modern life, might have been able in times long ago to track animals while hunting and might be able to learn to do it now. A wine connoisseur would make a good student, or a celebrity chef.

The dog is so much better because of its evolution as a hunting carnivore. Although the dog's eyesight is not so good with shape and colour, it is highly sensitive to movement, even very tiny movements, which is how those stage professors train their intellectual dogs to count. Also, the dog's hearing has a much wider range of frequencies and works at much lower volumes than a human's, but sight and sound alone do not ensure success for the hunter on the ground and so the dog has come to lead with its nose, to explore and explain the world with its sense of smell foremost. Someone the dog knows can walk along a path, followed by a dozen strangers carefully stepping in the same footprints, before they all peel off and hide. The dog, trained to do it, will track along the path and follow the smell he knows.

Cass would not be as good at scenting as a bloodhound or a basset, which were bred for the job, but then a basset wouldn't be much good at keeping a criminal in a corner, and that was a much bigger and more important difference.

By the end of the course, Cass would sit perfectly still and not move until he heard 'Come out or I will send the dog', and he would find the man wherever he was in the wood, up a tree or under a bush, and whatever the weather, and he would sit and bark, bouncing on his front paws until Joe arrived, and together they would escort the prisoner from his hiding place.

He would do it indoors too, as well as in woods, on the exercise they called 'building search, open and hidden person'. Good buildings were hard to find. The ideal was somewhere large, rambling and empty, owned by someone who didn't mind a lot of policemen and mad dogs tearing around. Arrangements were always temporary. Development or demolition would invariably spoil things, as would soon be the case with a particular disused mental hospital, previously a convalescent home for wounded soldiers in World War One, before that a Victorian workhouse.

History or no, it was perfect for open-and-hidden-persons. They were beyond open person, Biro thought, so he'd go hide. It was Solo's turn first, and then two more of the dogs had a go, so Cass was very agitated by the time the game came around to him. Off went Biro down a long corridor, doing his fine imitation of the Morecambe and Wise end-of-show exit dance with double arm movements and high heel kicks. The ground floor had been one large hall with kitchens, sculleries and so on leading off. Now it was a warren of rooms large and small, connecting or not. Biro went through four rooms leaving the doors open, up some stairs, down some more stairs, across a corridor, and into a gents lavatory where he slipped quietly into one of the traps, closed the door and stood on the seat.

Joe let Cass off the lead and he shot off, skidding on the old lino as he attempted a full-speed sharp left through the first doorway. He was through the next and the next before Joe had even reached the first. Then there was barking. Cass was barking, and how, but too soon to have found Biro.

Joe caught up to find the dog facing a blank wall, sitting, speaking, paws bouncing as if he were smack in front of his quarry, but there was nothing. There wasn't even a picture stuck up. It was a blank partition wall in faded white emulsion but Cass was giving it hell. He could see something there, or smell something, and he kept his famous speak going while Joe tried to work out what it could be.

'There's nothing there, Cass,' he said. 'Where is he?' Cass barked even louder and bounced even more. 'Cassius. Where is he?' said Joe, firmly.

Cass stopped barking and looked at Joe with that puzzled, disappointed expression on his face. Where is he? What's the fool on about? I've just told him 'where is he'.

The two of them hadn't done the multiple criminal exercises yet. Cass had only ever tried to find and speak with one prey to hunt and he'd found, so what was up?

Joe put Cass on the lead, led him into the next room, let him off again and said 'Where is he?' in as commanding a tone as he could manage, relying on Cass's habit of never backtracking. Sure enough, off he chased again. Joe was greatly relieved. Things were restored to normal.

Cass ran up the stairs, down the stairs, and into the gents lavatory, which was empty. The doors to all four WCs were shut, but behind one was Biro. Cass knew which one, of course, and sat down looking at it, but not barking. Barking at a blank wall, which was the same as a door, was apparently not approved of.

At the debrief outside, Cass's strange behaviour was much discussed. 'I bet he's never done that before,' said one. 'Maybe he saw a ghost,' said another. Biro said nothing, but that lunchtime, back at the school, he came into the locker room with an old copy of the local paper.

'Here, Joe, read this. And remember what I've told you a thousand times. Always trust your dog.'

Their morning's building, the workhouse/convalescent home/mental hospital, was scheduled for conversion to luxury apartments, which plan had drummed up a lot of local opposition and, with that, coverage in the local press. A reporter had managed to discover the grandson of one of the wounded soldiers from the Great War, who had heard his grandfather tell of his memories of his time at the convalescent home. He had been asleep one night when he woke up and sat up in bed all of a sudden. The room, although large enough for six beds, had only a small window set high in the wall, without curtains. Through it came a shaft of moonlight. The other five beds were unoccupied at that moment. Convalescent soldiers, notwithstanding their wounds, were often quite capable of extramural adventures that kept them out until all hours.

While our stay-at-home soldier stared around for a reason for his wakefulness, a figure with big mutton-chop whiskers appeared. He was dressed in top hat and frock coat and seemingly needed no recourse to either of the doors that let into the room. He consulted his fob watch, shook his head in irritation, turned and went through one of the doors but without opening it. He simply shimmied through as if there was nothing there.

'What did your grandfather think of that?' the reporter wanted to know. 'Ghost,' was the reply. Obviously. This reporter, clearly one destined for greater things, then tracked down one of the nurses from the building's days as a mental hospital. She had the same story, except it was the patients who had seen it and told her about it and, well, they were mental, weren't they, so nobody took any notice, not even when it had allegedly happened four or five times. They were handing the story on, the patients, you see. They thought they'd seen it. No such thing as ghosts, though, was there?

Biro gave them something of a lecture that afternoon. 'The indication when the dog finds may be only a small twitch, or a wag of the tail. He won't bark every time. He'll bark, or should bark, when he finds a human, but not necessarily for an inanimate object. The handler must watch his dog and know his dog. Every dog has his own twitch and you must be able to spot it. All right, now we're going to try something special that we always keep to near the end. You've done open-wood search with a man up a tree, you've done building-search. You've done chase-and-stand-off dozens of times, which we're now going to develop into chase-and-attack, where the suspect keeps on running. The danger here is that once the dog is encouraged to bite, will he ever want to stand off again? If the suspect does stop after the dog starts the chase, the dog has a decision to make. Does he convert to a stand-off, containing by barking, or does he carry on and bite anyway?

'The first phase is exactly the same. I will appear from

nowhere, you will shout your pathetic challenges – I have to say I particularly liked "Hey, you with the moustache, come here" – and I will walk away as any criminal would. You shout, "Stand still or I'll send the dog", and again because I keep going, and you set the dog away with "Hold him". All right so far? Now, instead of standing still as ordered, as I would in a stand-off, I break into a trot. I have in my hand a hessian sleeve. I let the dog catch me up and we have a tuggy game, and you catch me up and I give you the sleeve and you have a tuggy game.

'Like I said, we have to make sure that the dog knows the difference between a chase-and-stand-off, and a chase-and-attack. We don't want him attacking innocent people, and there's more of them about than you think. So we'll do a stand-off after a couple of chase and tuggy, then I'll put the sleeve on and get him to bite, and so on. Right. Who's first?'

Joe had no doubts about what Cass would be inclined to do in that situation and he was proved right, but the dog had to learn. In reality, he was unlikely to find a serious criminal stopping, standing there, expecting the dog to sit and wag its tail, but suspects were by no means always serious criminals. Completely innocent bystanders, in the wrong place at the wrong time, had the right to expect better treatment from the police that were supposed to be their protection. There was also the practical need for it to be done perfectly if Cass was to pass out with honours, to show he was entirely disciplined, and the equally compelling need not to be outshone by the other teams on the course.

There were furious, screaming, vehement shouts of 'Leave!'

when Cass did the other thing in the stand-off and, in his excitement, grabbed the arm of the fleeing criminal who had stopped, and Joe would berate the dog in loud and angry tones, making it clear who was top dog in this pack, Joe, and who was number two dog. Number two dog's response was to slide away in a sulk and not look Joe in the eye for some minutes.

After a few good chase-and-attacks, the hessian sleeve was ditched in favour of the leather one, much more tight fitting, more like an unprotected arm – and the dog had to bite harder to hang on to it.

When the dog was biting and holding in a chase-and-attack, he had to let go on 'Leave', walk away a few yards and go down while the handler searched the man. Eventually, Joe would get Cass to bark on a signal, by patting the criminal's outstretched arms during the search, and all three would march prettily back along the training field, criminal in front. It was a matter of management, of proving that the dog was under orders and that he had self-control. In training, the proof could be demonstrated, and on duty, in the big bad world, Cass would show again and again that he understood completely the difference between a running criminal and one who had been running but had stopped. He could not be blamed if he didn't know the difference between a running criminal and a running idiot.

The examination at the end of the course was not so much a test to fail, or a display to impress judges with technical merit and artistic impression, as a means to decide who had the top dog. More weighty was the police officer's confidence – 'Do I think I can go out on duty with this dog?' – and, most important of all was Biro's say-so. Thus would they all get their certificates, but who was going to be top of the form?

It was generally acknowledged to be between Zero, Dave Archer's snake in the grass, and Cassius, Joe Sleightholm's hairy monster. Both dogs were good at everything, although Zero had to give way slightly on agility, which meant that PC Archer had to find a little edge somewhere to counteract that. He thought he'd found it on the simple retrieve. When he thought Joe wasn't looking, he rubbed both ends of the dumb-bell with spit. If Cass picked it up by the end rather than the middle he'd lose points.

Joe saw and, when Dave really wasn't looking, swapped dumb-bells. Cass did it perfectly, Zero picked his up by one end. 'Has he ever done that before?' said Joe.

'You cheating bastard,' said Dave.

The traditional last day began with a trip to the seaside and concluded with a meal at one of the restaurants in Clufford with a private room, generally not the same one as the previous course had been to. Such recent memories could cause restaurants to find their private rooms already fully booked for the date mentioned.

It was still the off-season for tourists, so the beaches would have no dog restrictions. There would be miles and miles of golden sand wherever they chose to go, assuming they could agree on a choice. There were the usual arguments about whether to go east or west, to Saltburn, Whitby, Scarborough, Filey, Bridlington, or to Morecambe, Blackpool, Lytham, Southport.

Biro had informed them that he was coming and that he favoured Whitby, on the grounds that the tide was suitable that day, being low at noon while it was low four hours earlier at Morecambe, and the fish and chips were better.

They went in the big dog van: six dogs, six chattering kids and their urbane and liberal teacher Biro, on the school outing. It was a fine day as they drove into town at about half-past ten, headed for the west side and found a place to park on the Khyber Pass. The tide was as Biro had predicted, well on the way out, leaving them a three-mile-long stretch of beach to Sandsend. A bracing walk in the fresh sea breeze and the bright spring sunshine was just what the men wanted, especially as they knew there'd be a pint or two at The Hart before a quick march back for fish and chips.

They all let their dogs off the lead and away they went in joyous romp, chasing in circles, diving into the sea, running after balls and so on, except for Joe. He had to keep Cass on the lead and stay at the back of the troupe, the two outcasts, the two party poopers who might be potentially the best man-and-dog pairing in the force but with a dog that couldn't be let loose among his fellows without a battle ensuing. Biro noticed a glum Joe trying to look as if he didn't care, and dropped behind.

'Poor little Aggie, the one at the back,' he said.

'What?'

'Marriott Edgar. There's a famous seaside place called Blackpool. And poor little Aggie, the one at the back, she were one second too late. Don't you know any poetry?'

'Not my strongest suit, Biro. I remember that one about the highwayman came riding, up to the old inn door.'

'Every cloud has a silver lining, Joe,' said Biro. 'There's no such thing as a free lunch.'

'First it's poetry, then it's philosophy. Thank you for the kind words, Socrates.'

'What I mean is, you've got a brilliant dog there, Joe. All right, he doesn't like other dogs. All right, you can't join in the kiss-me-quickery with the other children. But you, Joe, and that dog, you are going to be something else.'

'Biro. You're a star. Now, tell me, what exactly is kiss-me-quickery?'

Joe and Cass slowed down until the others were far enough ahead for Cass not to be bothered. Off the lead he could be as happy as any dog, chasing balls, chasing seagulls and enjoying the open spaces, the beach being empty on an April weekday, except that he would not go in the sea. The sea was made of water. No matter how it glittered in the sunshine, no matter how much fun there looked to be in the foaming waves, it was water. QED.

Staying so far behind meant missing out on the crack in the pub too. The rest were about to set off back when Joe and Cass turned up, so Joe had one pint on his own sitting outside before resuming. 'Never mind, Cass,' he said. 'We don't care. Well, we do really, but there's no such thing as a free cloud.'

La Perugia in Clufford was the designated hot spot for the evening, with preamble at The Horse and Trumpet. The objective, naturally, was to get Biro drunk and to this end numerous beer-drinking games were devised, and various competitions organised with drinking penalties, but Biro was up to everything they tried. Every trap they laid, he saw through it or had seen it before. In any case, he was a prodigious beer drinker. Some of his pupils were quite proficient themselves in the consumption of the juice of the barley but none could match Biro pint for pint.

Nemesis was at hand, however. Glen Conway, he who had arranged the pub trip to the city, had made a few enquiries. He had discovered that Biro could stay up all night on beer and whisky but show him a small glass of Bulgarian Merlot or Chilean Cabernet Sauvignon, let him sniff the cork of a bottle of St Emilion or Côtes du Rhone, and he was anybody's. The owner of La Perugia, who was not an Italian but an Armenian called Hampartsumian, and a devout believer in being friendly with the police force, had been thoroughly briefed. Yes, the restaurant normally had Nastro Azzurro, and Moretti too, but the delivery hadn't arrived so they were all going to have wine from the grape when it is red, starting with a couple of bottles on the house.

'I'm not having any of that Valpolly stuff,' said Biro. 'Bad for you. Upsets the system.'

'But Mr Biro,' said Hampartsumian, 'this is not Valpolicella. This is Montepulciano d'Abruzzo, with much more refinement. She is purely for drinking pleasure, to accompany my food, and you will try a glass like this with your antipasto. Buon appetito.'

The glasses were large and soon drained. Bottles were ordered in threes. Plates of salami, Parma ham and olives disappeared, followed by cannelloni, by which time Biro was well away.

'Monty, what did he say? Any road, it's a drop o' good as my father used to say. No harm in it at all. Grape juice. Full of meaty goodness. With blackberry notes. Aye, I'll have another, why ever not? What's up, Joe? Got the twitch? Drop o' good, this. Have you had some?'

Side bets were laid. Six to four against falling off his chair. Even money, head-butting his saltimbocca. Two to one, unable to climb into a taxi on his own. Joe, who had taken the bet on what he called 'being taxily challenged', argued that he shouldn't pay out when Biro did indeed prove to be sufficiently incapable. His argument was that the bet assumed the cause of disability to be pissedness alone, and not compounded by Biro seeing the two steps out of the toilet as one and ending up semi-conscious on the carpet with his head in a bar stool.

CHAPTER SIX

THE START OF SOMETHING BIG

The daffodils were out, Cassius was shedding his winter coat, they were heading for a week's leave at home and so it seemed like a good idea to give the dog his first bath. At the training school, inside a small shed made of clear corrugated plastic there was a concrete trough tiled in beige, except for the bottom and the draining-board shelf to one side, which had black textured tiles to stop a dog from slipping.

It corresponded roughly to a large but narrow Belfast sink, about a yard long, half that wide and a little less deep, designed to provide enough room, but not too much, for a police officer to bathe his German Shepherd. There was a heavy-duty shower head, shampoo and medicated stuff to clean the skin of excess sebum, the fatty secretion that – in this breed of dog as with teenage boys – can produce unpleasant spots and eruptions.

There were certain measures that Joe could take to minimise the battle he saw coming. He had the bath half-filled ready, with warm but not hot water, and kept the tap running slowly to replace the water that would surely be shipped out. He would try his hardest not to allow water in Cass's ears, which would trigger a shake. Beyond that, it had to be a businesslike procedure: get dog thoroughly wet using tin jugs provided; shampoo and rinse; medicate and rinse; rinse again even more thoroughly with the shower; try drying with towels (probably not much use) and with the blow-dryer (dog may not like it).

As every dog lover knows, there are two types of dog: those who enjoy water and those who loathe it. This one, this Cassius, was a loather. Except when tracking or otherwise on duty, he would rather walk across hot coals than step in a puddle, but his trust in Joe was now total.

Few things can affect the heart of the dog handler as much as seeing his dog unhappy through following that trust. Most ordinary, non-police-trained dogs might have leaped out of the bath as soon as they went in. Cass obediently and trustingly stayed and, as Joe began pouring on the jugs of warm water, all the time telling Cassius how it was good for him and he'd come to like it after a while, the miserable look in the dog's eyes and his slouching, tormented demeanour said it all. Why, Cassius wanted to know, were such indignities being heaped upon him? What had he done to deserve this humiliation?

After the fourth or fifth jug, Cass refused to look at Joe the Betrayer any more. Even worse, The Man Previously Known As Friend went further and began frothing up the shampoo. Cass had had enough. He gave a huge shake and, while Joe tried to dodge the shower, made a dash for freedom. Joe grabbed him in a bear hug and kept him prisoner, resolving that the next bath would occur in the summer, when he could wear swimming trunks.

Joe kept one hand firmly on Cass's scruff for the rest of the procedure, pulling the plug, which was side-mounted in the trough so the dog didn't put his paw in it, and rinsing with the shower until he had a very dejected, soaking wet but squeaky clean dog standing in an empty bath.

'Standing' was hardly the word. So much water was trapped in his coat, and so much coat was there, that poor Cass was having trouble bearing up under the strain. With a load many times the usual, his legs were buckling. In such a state he had no inclination to jump from his torture chamber, so Joe had to half lift, half lever him out. One huge shake got rid of a large part of the water. To celebrate, Cass ran over to the nearest kennel and barked his annoyance and disappointment at the surprised inmate, another GSD, which barked back.

Joe called Cass and tried a towel, with no noticeable effect. It was time for the blower. The dog sat, compliant, water running from his coat on to the floor in rivulets. At the sound of the machine, like an industrial-quality hair dryer, he looked alarmed. At the first touch of its hot breeze, he was off. He wasn't having that – no way, matey. Never trust a copper.

Well, all right, it was a fine day, the field beside the school was recently mown, so Joe spent the next hour throwing a ball for Cassius until the running had dried him and tired him at the same time, and provided fun sufficient for Cassius to forgive his old pal Joe for that terrible ordeal.

Now that he was dry, Cassius was twice the size. He looked

like he'd been bouffed and pouffed by a team of twenty ladies' hairdressers. No best-of-breed at the sheep show could have been woollier. The creamy mane around his aristocratic head would have been the envy of every lion, from Aslan to the one that roars for MGM.

The upside of the process was Joe having to brush him, and Joe knew it would be a long old job. There would be a mountain of hair, all that extra winter warming coming out in handfuls, and Cass would love it and Joe would be exhausted, and at the end there would be the most magnificent, most handsome German Shepherd dog that Joe or anyone else had ever seen.

Regardless of his standing as supermodel, Cassius still had the standard police apartment to live in, back at Joe's house, but not for long. Plans had been laid to build a terrace, with patio and barbecue, and two adjacent kennels draining directly to the main. Meanwhile, Cassius had to settle in, get completely used to the family being around and understand that there was one borderline he could not cross: the threshold into the house. Over time, Cassius would develop his own compromise on this. He would place his front paws over the threshold but go no further.

Cassius and Leila had met but not been on a walk together. Joe bundled them both into the back of his hatchback one morning and headed for the hills. Cass was a natural traveller and Leila was used to it, so there was no bother between them, but as soon as they jumped out and set off walking, the jockeying for primacy began. Cassius quickly showed that he would not tolerate another dog in his place, close to Joe's left side. When Leila tried to get in there, she was bullied out of it.

In later weeks and months, if Joe held one of his daughters by his left hand, Cass would force his way between them.

On this first walk, on a fine spring day with new life bursting out all around, Leila eventually ceded left field to Cass, after about ten attempts to dislodge him, but still felt she had a point to make. She hung back a little. After a minute or two, she sneaked up and nipped Cass on the back leg. He was shocked. He didn't know how to handle it.

If ever a dog could be said to be smirking, that dog was Leila. She waited until normal rhythms had been resumed, sneaked up again and bit Cass's other leg. Joe said nothing, interested to see how that little power struggle would resolve itself, and after the fourth nip Cassius turned and charged. Leila spun away and ran in a wide circle with Cassius tucked in her slipstream. When she changed direction, he took over the lead in another circle going the opposite way. Round and round they went, clockwise, anticlockwise, jinking like chased rabbits, having the most enormous amount of fun. Joe watched and marvelled, and thought how shrivelled and prune-like must be the souls of those senior officers who stated the force's clear preference for dog handlers to keep only their police dog and no other.

Momentarily tired, the two dogs settled back into the orderly business of going for a walk with the boss, Cass close to Joe's left leg, Leila a couple of yards behind or in front, depending. Cassius's reluctance to leave open his position, in case Leila should try to take it again, meant that he missed out on a lot of sniffing and exploring. Leila roamed, investigating, downloading all the curiosities, making whatever subliminal mental notes dogs make while employing their sense of smell so many times more sensitive than a human's.

After a while, Cass got fed up with this. He thought it was time for another whirligig chase so he broke away, gave Leila a nip on her back leg, and ran off. Leila ignored him. When he came and did it again, she ignored him again, and doubled the snub by placing herself close up on Joe's left side. Outmanoeuvred by the smarter and older female, the male resorted to brute strength and shoved Leila out of his favoured spot, but that didn't matter. Leila was satisfied with her victory. Henceforth, she would decide when there would be whirligigs, not Cassius.

And so the week's holiday passed pleasantly by. On the walks, Joe tried to keep Cass up to scratch with activities similar to the excitement, play and rewards of those intensive training weeks. If there was a stile and a fence, or a five-bar gate, Cass would have to find his own way over. They did some tracking and retrieving, and finding small articles, and Cassius became used to the comings and goings at home, except that he could not fathom the sparrows.

These would hang around his run, waiting for an opportunity to slip in through the mesh to pick up unconsidered trifles from his food bowl. When he seemed to be asleep in his kennel, in they would fly, and Cassius would dash at them, and they would fly away. He would bark his warning, that little feathered irritants would not be tolerated, and slide back into his kennel. A few minutes later the same thing would happen, and again, until there were no more crumbs from the rich dog's table of sufficient interest to warrant such risky raids, and Cass would have some peace at last, until the next time, or until a hot-air balloon came over. Some dogs bark at the moon, some at statues in the park, some at an old carrier bag blown on the wind until it sticks in the hedge. Cassius barked at hot-air balloons. He hated them with a passion. Had one ever run out of gas and landed in Joe's garden, Cass would have broken any chains to get at it.

The family also learned that Cass did not like hugs. He loved being brushed, and liked a fuss being made, but not hugs. He seemed embarrassed. He wriggled out when it was tried and went off to create a diversion.

For Joe, Cass was the element that completed his life. He had his family, their home, and the occasional football match and visit to the pub. Add the dog and there was no time, or inclination, for anything else. In any case, 'owning' a police dog was not like owning a pet. Police training never stopped. A Sunday-morning walk included heelwork. A game in the garden might dissolve into ball chasing, but it would have started with the home-size version of property square. If you were a total dog man like Joe, and a one-man dog like Cass, the relationship developed a mutual dependency, as close as any marriage, of minds and hearts.

The start of the following week saw another big change in life's routines. It was work – police work, real work, not training – and home for a large part of the day became the police dog van. There were three vans on the force, between six handlers. On duty, the van was kennel for Cass and office, café and operational HQ for Joe. This was especially so on nights, when the van was never left except for action, and by the end of the week it was ready for the big clean the handlers always gave it before passing it on to a colleague.

The body of the van was lined in washable plastic and divided along its length by a wood partition, so there was room for two dogs. The traditional material for floor mats, to stop the dogs sliding about, was conveyor-belt rubber. Dogs could get out via the cage doors at the back, or the sliding partition at the front, which separated dogs and men. There was a compartment for kit (waterproofs, boots and so on) and that was it. Police radio in the front, of course, and there you had it: home from home. In the summer, the handler might leave the back doors open while parked up, waiting for something to happen, but no one with any sense would go near an open van with a dog inside, even a caged one. Mobile kennel, office, HQ, whatever: it was territory and would be fiercely defended.

Jack Robinson brought the van round for Joe to take over. He'd been on nights, as Joe would be. It might prove a gentle introduction for Cass, or it might not.

'You may notice,' said Jack, 'that there is a piece missing from the passenger seat. I've put in for a new one.' Joe nodded but said nothing. Jack was obviously bursting to tell the story.

'I'm sitting in a lay-by, it's raining, when this car goes by, steady like, with the offside wheels glued to the white line.' Such means of navigation were well known and invariably led directly to a charge of driving while tired and emotional. 'So I pulls out and stops him. No need to call for the alcometer. As a newt, he is. I've only got the van so he gets in the passenger seat. So, we're driving along, conversation not exactly flowing when, all of a sudden, the bastard grabs the handbrake, yanks it vertical, the van does a Torvill and Dean, and he opens his door and starts to climb out.

I slide open the partition behind me as I try to prevent my man becoming an escaped prisoner. He was quite a big fellow and he'd taken a dislike to me.'

'What, did he whack you?'

'Tried to. But Jaffa jumps out from behind me, lands bang on top of me and rams my face into the steering wheel, doesn't recognise the prisoner for what he is and scrabbles across his head and out onto the road. There, Jaffa's looking all over for the departing criminal which, according to his knowledge and experience, should be someone hot-footing it across the meadow with a hundred yards' start. I shouts, "Hold him", and Jaffa turns and makes a lunge through the open door, sinks his teeth into the passenger seat and rips a bloody great lump out of it.'

'He missed the bloke and bit the seat instead?'

'Well, yes, and the silly sod of a prisoner still tried to get out of the van, which is how I ended up standing next to a naked man down at the nick, with the desk sergeant making all kinds of funny noises as he took down the details while trying not to laugh.'

'Naked? Why was he naked?'

'Well, he wasn't. Not entirely. He had his shoes and socks on, and he had a trouser waistband complete with belt and belt loops, but that was all. Jaffa had stripped the lot. Must have been trying to get rid of the taste of the van seat.'

'Blimey. Does Jaffa take Y-fronts as well? And what about his wedding tackle?'

'No, he doesn't touch underwear of any kind. He's been properly trained. But this bloke wasn't wearing any. He was on his way to a certain club and wanted to provide easy access. And even when Jaffa had finished, there wasn't a mark on him. So the sergeant calls the doctor and says the guy has to have a blood test to confirm his reading because the station machine isn't working. And he looks at me and says, "What am I going to put here about the prisoner's clothes, when your dog's eaten them?" I just shrugged and said, "I don't know. He's never done that before."'

No such incidents came the way of Joe and Cassius on their first tour of duty together. A week of nothing doing, and doing nothing, must have felt strange to Cassius. Certainly it felt like a week of failure to Joe and, despite his efforts to make up for it with tracks and other games, the tension, the boredom, the frustration, communicated in a tangle of emotions to Cass, who would have sensed that this, this life, wasn't it. Sitting in a police dog van in the dark was not his sole purpose, even if the long hours were occasionally punctuated with a piece of sandwich. Sardine was nice, he liked that, and ham – no mustard – and cheese and sweet pickle, but there had to be something else, and the first sign of it came early in the second week. The pair were on days. Start at eight, cheerio to family, have breakfast, into the van, turn on the radio.

'Alpha Golf Zero Three, urgent. Vehicle is failing to stop.'

'CD to patrols. Urgent. Golf Three behind BMW car Romeo seven niner five Papa Victor Alpha, south towards Rickaby from Aldborough. Vehicle is failing to stop. Patrols to make.'

'Speed sixty. Wrong side of the road passing The Quiet Woman.'

'Vehicle sixty passing Quiet Woman, still towards Rickaby.'

All this was happening no more than three or four miles away from Joe Sleightholm and Cassius. Such chases often ended in a crashed and/or abandoned stolen car with villains sprinting into the distance. This could be Initiation Day. Joe tried to book on, to tell the control room he was on the case, couldn't get a word in edgeways and set off anyway.

'Golf Three. Vehicle committed eastbound A ten forty. Speed sixty.'

'Tango Golf Zero Two. Turned on to A ten forty. Vehicle two hundred yards.'

The driver of Golf Three, the section car, must have allowed the traffic car, Tango Golf – doubtless with lights, horns and everything going – to take over the chase. The much more powerful pursuer had swung in after the BMW, surely a stolen car, now heading away from Clufford, away from the suburbs, towards open country.

'Tango Golf Zero Two. Vehicle left into White Horse Common Road. Speed sixty plus.'

Unless they doubled back or made some other major route change, the thieves would soon be in a maze of country lanes, unable to put any distance between themselves and the traffic car, which was driven by someone who had passed every advanced driving course there was to be passed. If the thieves were city boys, joy riders, they'd be nosing through a hedge or a stone wall in no time.

Joe made some calculations in his head, predicted where the chase was most likely to end, and went for it. He was barely a quarter of a mile away when it happened.

'Tango Golf Zero Two. Vehicle in ditch, White Horse Common, east side. Bailing, bailing. Two on foot.'

To Joe, the traffic cop's voice sounded disappointed, crestfallen, and when he turned up a minute or two later he saw why. The cop in question may well have been athletic in his youth but that was no longer the case. Out of his car, in his yellow fluorescent jacket (size extra large) and his driving shoes, he was lumbering up a ploughed incline like an elderly prop forward unwillingly attending a line-out at the end of a hard match. It was only a slight incline but the recent rain had made the going soft to very bad. This affected the hunted as well as the hunter, however, and they were not so far away as they might have been on good ground.

For Cassius, the scene could hardly have been less like training school. Some dogs, even graduates with honours, simply refused to perform when suddenly faced with such foreign circumstances. For the first time, the quarry was not an instructor or student from the course acting the goat. The ground was not the usual cropped meadow, nor the Ten Acre Wood. No, thank you, boss. Don't like it. Don't understand it.

Joe had been wishing for some action; he might have wished for something simpler, because the first task seemed to be to get the fat copper out of the way without Cassius biting him. Setting the dog off on a chase meant, naturally, that he would go for the nearest target first. If the target stood still, with any luck Cassius would do a stand-off and bark. If the target kept going, well, he'd be putting in for a new uniform jacket and trousers as well as a yellow fluorescent.

'Stand still or I'll send the dog,' shouted Joe at the top of his voice to the tubby yellow trundler, and 'Hold him,' as quietly as he could to the excited dog. Cassius set off at a lick. The traffic man turned and saw the great hairy hound from hell bounding towards him, ears flat. 'Stand still!' screamed Joe again and, being an experienced officer who had seen Cassius types before, he did exactly that.

Joe, running, allowed himself a smile of pride as his fabulous, brilliant dog did the perfect stand-off, barking, bouncing, but not biting. The two thieves, getting further and further away, took a quick look over their shoulders when they heard Cassius and found they could run a little faster.

'Sorry about that,' said Joe, catching up with dog and Traffic. The portly one may have wanted to say, 'That's all right, mate, quite understand', but couldn't actually speak.

Cassius, with his fat man seemingly arrested, was pleased with himself. At training school, a successful exercise was followed by a reward, so where was it? 'Good boy, come,' said Joe. Yes, praise was part of it. Cassius stopped barking, sat on Joe's left side, and looked like he'd won dog of the month.

Joe went on one knee by Cass, pointed at the fleeing figures on the horizon, and said, 'Hold him,' with urgency in his voice. Cassius barked, got up, sat again, got up, turned to the traffic cop, barked, sat again. What was going on?

'Hey you, this is the police, stand still or I'll send the dog. Hold him, hold him,' cried Joe, setting off himself and pointing with his right arm outstretched. Cassius still didn't get it. He jumped around as if expecting Joe to throw him a ball. 'Hold him, Cass, for ****'s sake!' screamed Joe.

They were at the summit of a low hill. There was little to

impede their view, and coming up the other side was a policeman, presumably the one who'd been driving the section car. Sensibly, he halted to watch events unfold.

The spectator interest was being provided on the one hand by PC Sleightholm and his bouncing dog, recent captors of one of their own, and by the two car thieves, now several hundred yards in the lead, crossing a small brick bridge and taking a short breather, presumably to decide which way to run, then disappearing from view. That pause, that little stop, was enough. Cassius saw them, clicked, and was away.

The forces of law and order converged on the little bridge. Of the men, Joe was there first and looked down onto a canal in a cutting, with a muddy, overgrown towpath. Cassius was haring along it, past a moored narrowboat. A man on the deck, possibly an ageing refugee from Woodstock, threw whatever he was smoking in the canal and hurriedly went below.

Joe, pelting along the towpath, for some reason did not shout 'Stand still' to the two thieves. Later, in his report, he would say that he had shouted but they were too far away to hear.

Cassius was nearly on top of the tiring lads when he checked in his stride. Something was wrong. Something in his brain did not compute.

'Hold him,' shouted Joe, panting hard, eighty yards or more behind. Cassius kept running, but not with his previous certainty. What was the matter?

'It's the arms,' said Joe to himself. Of course. In training, the dog is made to go for the right arm, the one with the protective sleeve on it. Here, in real life for the first time, Cassius could see the right arms well enough, but they were water-side. He couldn't have thought it through – If I jump for that arm I'll take us both into the canal and I've not been trained in swimming stand-offs – but there was still a puzzle. And he hated water.

'Hold him,' shouted Joe again, and for Cassius the puzzle was resolved. He put in half a dozen faster, longer strides and bit the nearest lad hard in the backside. As Cass adjusted his grip, the lad yowled in pain and fear and the other, the front runner, jumped in the canal. His wounded mate, struggling free from Cassius and shrieking obscenities the while, jumped in after. The water came up to their armpits. One, the unbitten, thrashed at the surface with his hands as if the spray might keep Cassius on the bank. The second, a pain in his bum, made wailing noises. Cassius, his job as clearly and finally done as any job could be, turned happily away and began trotting back towards Joe.

'Watch him!' screeched Joe, more urgently than Cass had ever heard before and, glory be, that dog turned on a sixpence, roared back to the bewildered and besodden thieves, slid to a halt in a shower of sand and gravel and, bouncing on his paws, showed his charges once more what he would do to them if they tried anything.

Joe arrived, quietened Cass with a 'Good lad, good lad', and heard cheering. Coming across the field were two more police, two traffic cops of long standing and well known to Joe, who had arrived during the show, watched the denouement, and were now proceeding at regulation pace towards it. Joe made the arrests, one at a time, with handcuffs, borrowing a set from the section-car cop, who had turned up beaming all over his face.

The two traffic officers couldn't stop laughing and shaking their heads in amazement, as they took possession of the thieves and began making their way back to their car. Cassius, meanwhile, rewardless apart from a little praise, forgotten in the arrest formalities, with his excitement turbocharged by all the laughter and merriment, ran up the canal bank, ran down again, and bit the larger of the two traffic cops on the ankle.

Even that didn't stop him laughing. 'Just a love bite,' he said to Joe. 'Just a love bite.'

One problem with a dog like Cass would always be that he was liable to go for a police colleague, in uniform or not, if that police officer seemed to the dog to be misbehaving, which is to say, in most cases, running away. Or, if it happened to be the first person Cass saw after being instructed to go get, the dog would naturally assume that the first was the most wanted. His whole business was about people misbehaving, not what they were wearing. Being a dog, and therefore partly colour blind, Irish and Welsh rugby supporters would have looked the same to him. He could tell the difference between a man wearing a yellow jumper and a man wearing a blue one, but without further evidence, especially from his nose, he couldn't tell which side of the law each was on.

CHAPTER SEVEN

SUCH DOGS ARE DANGEROUS

There'd been a spate of armed robberies. They were small scale, amateurish, nobody had been shot, but the perpetrator was getting away every time. His routine was to dash into a village post office, or a small betting shop, or maybe a corner store, and stick a gun in the face of the person at the till. He'd take whatever there was, often not much, and if there was CCTV it was no help because he had a very nice line in disguises. Always he wore sunglasses, sometimes a Scottish Jimmy hat, sometimes a flat cap and false beard, sometimes an Ozzy Osbourne wig, but whatever he chose it was never threatening. He never wore a balaclava, for example. People he robbed said they didn't really think he would shoot them but they'd rather give him the money than take the risk.

One Saturday afternoon, the gunman tried something new: dressing as a woman. He wasn't especially tall or well built so he passed quite well in the greengrocer's shop as a rather plain, verging on the ugly, Sloane Ranger type with designer shades, neat blue jacket and skirt and silk headscarf, but his lack of familiarity with handbags let him down. He began speaking his opening lines, which was simple stuff about give me the money or else, while he was still fiddling with the catch on the bag to get his gun out. With the girl behind the counter staring in amazement, this strange-looking woman gave up the attempt, ran from the shop and headed for the railway station.

The greengrocer dialled 999. The station was a single-track branch line from Clufford to the coast, with trains mostly every hour in each direction. They passed at this station, the coast-bound train waiting for the other to go through, so the robber could be heading either way. He'd done his research, because the trains were due and he'd have had time to catch either except, the police's own research quickly revealed, there was maintenance work on the line that weekend and everyone was being taken by bus.

Both buses were stopped by the police and nobody was found who even vaguely resembled a cross-dressing armed robber, so Joe and Cass were called in. The trail was half an hour old by this time, but Cass was soon on to it. About five hundred yards from the station he found a neatly folded pile of clothing: a dark-blue skirt and jacket and a floral print headscarf, but no handbag. Joe was on the radio immediately. The robber was free, dressed in goodness knows what, and the dog was very keen to follow a rough, half-made road that led, Joe knew, to an empty farmstead, one waiting for the demolition boys to come along and start converting it into a neo-Georgian housing estate with flagpoles.

All available units were called in except for firearms, who were too far away just then to be any use.

With the place surrounded, Joe agreed to go in with his dog. It was no certainty their quarry was there in the farm, but if he was, he had his gun with him. Admittedly, reports gave the impression of a non-violent gunman but you never could be sure what a man in a corner might do. Joe could get himself shot. Cass could be shot. They were going to fields of fire and while Joe understood the risk and could feel the fear, Cass had no reason to hesitate for himself. He could smell Joe's unease, but that only made him more excited. Being able to smell fear in a friend didn't necessarily make a dog share it. Like the soldiers of Henry V, he stood like a greyhound in the slips, straining upon the start. The game – Cass's game, the game he was trained to play – was afoot.

The rest of the police, and there were quite a few of them, would slowly close in behind Joe, drawing the net tighter. He and Cass had a look at the cart-track. Cass had no doubts whatever. Here was the scent. The robber had gone to the farm. Displaying rather more caution than usual, and keeping Cass on the shortest possible line, they followed the road around a bend, a straight, another bend, and here was the farmyard.

The problem Joe had was where to start in his search of the buildings, and he was weighing this up with Cass sitting at his side, keeping under cover as best he could. Out of the corner of his eye, he saw a figure moving, running, keeping his head down, on the far side of the yard, behind a wall. Cass saw it too and wanted to go.

Joe shouted, 'Stand still or I will send the dog' and released Cass at the same moment. The dog leaped over the wall and two seconds later there was an almighty shout and scream. Joe hurried across the yard and through a gate, to be confronted by a horrifying sight. Facing him was a special constable of his good acquaintance, with one arm raised in the air, truncheon in hand, which he'd drawn in case he came across the man with the gun. On the special's back was a large hairy dog with his teeth fixed in the collar of the police-issue, heavy-duty black anorak. Cass was doing his best to rip the anorak from collar downwards and, by the sound of it, was slowly succeeding.

The dog was really excited and very difficult it was for Joe to get him off. Cass accepted Joe's praise as his due, because he had only done what he was trained to do.

'Didn't you hear me shout?' Joe asked the special.

'Well, yes, I did, but I never thought you were shouting at me.' Joe made a mental note to suggest a small insert into the training of special constables, indicating that police dogs cannot tell the difference between a moving police officer and a moving armed robber.

'Are you all right? Has he bitten you?' The special showed Joe two red furrows ploughed in his right arm, where Cass had begun his assault and where his teeth had slipped down the shiny, extra-tough material of the anorak. He'd raised his arm and truncheon out of the way, so Cass had run around behind and got hold of his collar. A much better grip and the stitching of the collar had given the dog a more satisfactory ripping.

'I saw our man running away from the farm but my radio had

packed up, so I thought I'd better chase after. I wasn't far behind, then I heard you shout so I thought you must have seen him.'

Joe settled Cass back into search mode and set off. It really didn't take long. Sleightholm's Law stated that it was a curious but well-established fact that a felon, when chased by a member of the public, will keep going and going in expectation of getting away because the chaser will give up. When chased by the police, this same felon will go to ground somewhere, hide himself and wait, knowing that the police are less likely to give up but might well pass by. Following Sleightholm's Law, the robber had crawled into a mixed bed of nettles and hardy perennials in what once had been the farmer's well-stocked garden. Cass barked and bounced and the man came out, having been assured he would not be mauled. He was wearing the strip of a big city football team and carrying a handbag.

'Play for them, do you?' said Joe. 'Let's have the bag.'

'Yeah, in my dreams,' said the man, passing the bag over. Inside was the gun, a real one. 'It's all right. It's not loaded. I never load it. I don't want to hurt anyone. It's bad enough robbing people without hurting them as well.'

A successful arrest of a troublesome robber would be no more than was expected at HQ. No medal would be issued for an unarmed dog tackling a gunman, whether the gun had been loaded or not. What might be noted was that the dog had ferociously attacked one of his allies, a uniformed officer, and two further incidents closely following this one very nearly ended Cass's career before it had really got going.

A certain furniture store in Clufford centre had a spacious area at the back where the van was kept. The Plan A of a certain pair of burglars was to break into the shop from the rear, load the choicest pieces into the van and make off in the transport so kindly provided, even though its proper ownership was identified all over it in large letters. They broke into the shop all right, thus triggering the alarm in the police station, and ran into the yard with a couple of very fine Moroccan carpets singing 'Fly Me to the Moon', but when they came to break into the van they found it already loaded with leather three-piece suites. Quickly switching to Plan B, they jumped in, started the engine with no trouble and drove away.

By the time the call went out, they could have been almost anywhere but PC Sleightholm, sitting in his dog van by a bridge over the motorway, saw the name of the furniture shop go past. The registration checked. It was the burglars. Joe radioed the control room and followed from a good distance. They turned down a minor road. Joe radioed again and his eager colleagues set up a roadblock at the obvious place, a T-junction a few miles further on, and waited. Joe asked everyone to give the dog a chance. If the quarry bailed out, no one was to give chase in front of Cass.

The burglars seemed in no hurry, just tootling along the road, and were clearly surprised when they saw the police cars parked up ahead because their first reaction was to put the foot down, aiming to barge their way through. They changed their minds almost immediately, slewed into the kerb, both leaped out on the passenger side and ran up the drive of a rather smart detached house.

Joe had pulled up on the driver's side of the van. By the time he got Cass out of the front hatchway, five bobbies and a sergeant were ignoring Joe's pleas and were thundering up the drive after the burglars.

Joe, last in the queue, cursed the enthusiasm of police officers everywhere who were so stupid that they wanted to arrest burglars. With Cass running free, he would try to overtake.

The owners of the house, an elderly couple, had been on their doorstep bidding farewell to friends when the new drama unfolded for them to watch. First the two villains went by at top speed, through the gap between garage and hedge and, by the sound of it, over the ten-foot fence at the back. Then, a phalanx of large policemen turned up, panting and not sure what to do next. The elderly couple and their supper guests assumed they were being raided, or at least had become unwitting parts of Operation Doomsday, shortly to feature the armed response unit and the riot squad. One of the women burst into tears, the other started screaming hysterically, her husband slapped her, she slapped him back, and the man whose house it was began shouting about Magna Carta and their rights as private citizens under common law to quiet enjoyment.

Then another very tall policeman arrived with a huge hairy hound that took one look at the assembled and noisy throng, decided that he had better go for the nearest one and bit him in the hand. Pity of it was, the nearest one was the sergeant.

'Yer bastard,' he said, pulling his hand away and raising it above his head.

'Down, Cass,' said Joe, quietly. 'And if it's all right with you, Sarge, I'll get after the burglars.'

While the sergeant restored order and calm, suggesting that perhaps the supper party had better reconvene for a soothing cup of tea or a glass of Wincarnis, Joe and Cass, unable to leap a ten-foot fence, had to run back down the drive and up a side entry to get into the passageway that ran along the backs of the houses. There were police here too, ruining any scent there might have been and Cass, still a little excited about biting the sergeant, couldn't settle to any strong line of enquiry. At the far end of the passageway was the edge of a golf course. This, Joe thought, must be the answer but, two hours later, Cass had unfortunately only proved two things. One: there were no furniture thieves on the golf course. And two: there were exceptions to Sleightholm's Law. Well, at least the police had got the van and contents back and were able to suggest to the shop owners that, if they were going to leave lorry loads of leather out at night, they might immobilise the transport.

For Cass, worse than biting the sergeant was to come, and not long after. Joe was running late for the start of his evening shift, coming back from a walk in the nearby woods with both the dogs and both the daughters. He remembered he'd nothing in the fridge for his sandwiches so, outside the village grocery shop, which called itself a delicatessen, he sat the two dogs down and gave the leads to Holly, then all of eight years old. The street was empty, he'd only be a minute. He went into the shop to find another customer, a cheery lady in her early thirties, dressed in a tracksuit, refusing the Caerphilly and the Lancashire because she especially wanted Wensleydale. As she turned and went out, a terrible thought crossed Joe's mind.

With a 'Back in two ticks' to the shopkeeper, he was through the door – but too late. The woman, seeing the two little girls and the two huge and apparently beautifully behaved dogs sitting beside them, had gone across to chat and give the dogs a pat. Cass, his duty clear and seeing himself in charge of the situation, had pre-empted any potential harm to those in his care by nipping behind the woman and biting her quite hard in the bottom.

There were drops of blood on the pavement. Holly was crying and so Harriet started crying too. Leila looked bemused. The woman looked composed, as if she had her plan of retribution worked out, and received Joe's flood of apologies with polite reserve. He took her details, rushed home with dogs and kids and went to work without any sandwiches.

The first thing he did was tell his boss, the officer who had everyday responsibility for the dog handlers: Sergeant McKay. Mac was a two-dog man, with a Springer drugs dog and a GSD, coincidentally called Brutus, which was another not conforming to the perfect breed profile. He had a squared-off snout that made him look like he'd run at high speed into something solid, such as a cathedral.

Sergeant McKay listened to the tale, took note of Joe's distress, which was increasing by the minute as he began to appreciate what was at stake here, and decided not to go upstairs, to Division and to the Chief Inspector in charge of the dog school – at least, not yet. He would try to resolve things by local negotiation: try to persuade the woman not to take matters any further, try to stop the apple cart before it rolled down the hill and smashed into a thousand pieces.

The unthinkable alternative was the incident reaching the top floor, pursued and reinforced by lawyers. It was only a little nip in the bottom, admittedly with blood drawn, but much could be made of it. If the woman turned out to be a belligerent, opportunistic and vindictive whinger, intent on substantial compensation for damage to her person and her mental health, and if she surrounded herself with learned friends of the blame-and-claim tendency, she could turn a relatively small thing into a disaster.

For Joe, that would mean an official verbal whipping and a posting back to standard duties. Of far more concern, to Joe and Mac, was the fate of Cassius. For doing no more than fulfilling his responsibilities as he saw them, he would be classified as a danger to the public. Yes, he had assisted materially in the arrest of an armed robber, but that was his job. That was what police dogs were supposed to do. What they were not supposed to do was bite police sergeants and women out buying cheese. The matter could be tidily resolved by classifying Cassius as beyond control, guilty of unacceptable behaviour, and so he would be taken to a place of execution.

Mac got in his car and went straight round to the woman's house, which was some miles away. *Oh Lord, let her not be the unforgiving sort.* Mac would be playing it by ear, but he was bound to offer her the opportunity of making an official complaint.

By a near-incredible stroke of coincidental luck, the woman had a brother who was a police-dog handler in the neighbouring force. She would make no complaint, and when Mac offered her financial compensation for her tracksuit, she told him it was a very old one. Her main expenditure had been on the iodine and Elastoplast, which had already been stored in the medicine cabinet. And, answering the unspoken question, she made Mac blush the deepest red by telling him she hadn't been wearing any.

'Oh, and before you say it, Sergeant, I know. He's never done that before.'

CHAPTER EIGHT

THROUGH THE
DEEDS OF MEN

'It's a histiocytoma,' said the vet.

'It's a whatter?' said Joe.

'Benign tumour. Nothing to worry about.'

'Nothing to worry about? It's on his nose. He's got a sodding great raspberry growing on his nose, the prime tool of his trade, and you say it's nothing to worry about?'

Joe was distraught. By now, Cass had proved that he could track like he was on rails. Like many animals he could smell fear, but he had also learned that the majority of sinners against the law of the land were less meticulous about their personal hygiene than those who trod the straight-and-narrow path of righteousness. Once he got that double aroma, of BO and alarm, he was like a missile on a wire.

He could sense his handler's excitement, pleasure and satisfaction in his performance, and it gave him the same emotions too. Take away the key to his performance, his nose, and what would be left? A dog that couldn't hack it any more, a frustrated and upset handler, a dog that didn't understand what had gone wrong, and another way to end a most promising professional and personal association.

'Constable. I told you. It's nothing. Don't panic, you'll excite the dog.'

In the old days, thought Joe, vets were called Jim or Steve or Douglas. Or Siegfried, come to that. The occasional lady vet could equally well have been a school headmistress or a racehorse trainer. Now, vets were called Emma, Tracey or, in this case, Tamsin. Joe Sleightholm, being of the slightly unreconstructed school of human relations, like so many in his line of work, tried his best to put his whole future in the hands of this young woman who, had she chosen a different career path, would have been very comfortable running an art gallery in Bond Street, or introducing *Newsnight* on BBC2.

'I'm going to anaesthetise him and remove the tumour. He'll need stitches.'

'Stitches?' said Joe. 'Will he have a scar?'

'Possibly. Now, if you want to be helpful, hold his head while I give him the anaesthetic. Can't you stop that growling?'

They were on days that week and half a day had been allocated for veterinary consultation. The other half was duty and for the first time Joe hoped they wouldn't get any business. He didn't want Cass bashing his nose on something and tearing the stitches. It might spoil his looks. When the inevitable call came in, it was to attend at a shopping mall where a man was brandishing a pitchfork, threatening to treat anyone who came near him in the same way as he'd treat a stook of hay. Joe didn't like the sound of it.

'But Sarge, he's already had an operation on his nose today. Can't you send somebody else?'

'Get on with it, you big tart.'

On the way there, Joe tried to work out how on earth he could deal with this. Obviously he couldn't let the dog go and have him double-pronged by a mad pitchfork wielder. There was nothing in the training manual under the heading 'Spears, assegais, swords and pitchforks'. His personal radio spoke.

'Here is a message for PC Big Tart, otherwise known as Zulu Charlie Four Zero. The pitchfork and its owner have been taken into custody by a WPC who is willing to offer training in unarmed disarming as regards long, sharp weapons.'

Joe was beginning to feel persecuted. First his marvellous dog was in line for the big sleep because he was biting all the wrong people. Now he was gaining Joe a reputation for being a namby pamby, a lonely little petunia in the onion patch. Oh well. Tomorrow was the drugs raid.

There was always good intelligence on dogs at raid briefings. Before the dangerous dog laws came in, every self-respecting drug dealer had a pit bull or a Tosa Inu (huge red Japanese mastiff), a Rottweiler or similar. They were mainly to intimidate the dealers' customers and make sure of prompt payment and honest transactions, but their secondary purpose was to defend raided premises and thus gain valuable hiding, escaping or dumping time for their miscreant owners. On one famous occasion, such a delay gave the drug dealer time to dash out into his back yard and hide a plastic bag of heroin where he had trained his dog to do its business. Alas for him, police familiarity with drug dealers provided a good education in the ways a cunning mind could work.

When a raid was being planned, the first mention of a dog, whether large, small, vicious bobby-eater or whatever, produced a call to a dog handler. They might well want to use a dog for searching but it wouldn't work very well until the other dog had been removed, so a dog handler was doubly necessary. Here could be seen the reluctance of police officers, otherwise quite prepared to disarm a drunk waving a broken bottle or risk being shot by an armed robber, to face a disagreeable, territorial, sharp-toothed canine. The dog handler, although a normal human being in every respect – including having an aversion to being bitten – was, by virtue of his trade, assumed to have magical powers over all dogs, not just his own. In fact, what he had was a protective sleeve as used in training, shin guards from the riot uniform worn back to front to protect against bites in the calf, which experience had shown to be a likely point for a pit bull to aim at, and a powder fire extinguisher.

The standard and traditional scenario: two burly PCs with sledgehammers knock down the door; dog handler minus dog pushed to the fore to be confronted by pit bull/Rottweiler/Tosa Inu frothing at the mouth; dog handler sprays dog with fire extinguisher; pit bull/Rotty/Tosa retires in shame, covered in white powder. It never seemed to occur to senior officers that a dog handler's training did not necessarily take in fire extinguishing and that burly sledgehammerers could do it equally well.

By the time Cass joined the front line, studies had been conducted after a quite different senior officer idly wondered what might happen if the fire extinguisher didn't work and a dog handler was badly bitten. In the age of litigation, a man or woman equipped only with training sleeve and shin pads might seek the advice of some highly paid Rumpoles. The RAF Regiment was the acknowledged leader in aggressive use of dogs and so help was sought from that quarter. When pursuing an intruder on an RAF base, the regimental dog handlers were liable to shoot at their target as well as send dogs developed to a very high pitch of fearless attack, but what especially interested the police investigators was the protective clothing the handlers wore in training. Rather than just a sleeve, these people made themselves an entire suit as part of their course. Going that far would not be necessary for police training, but such suits would be commissioned and would be kept at the dog school, ready to be issued as required.

Nothing else changed, however, and when the word 'dog' came up at the next drug-raid briefing, Joe Sleightholm received the call. This raid was to be mounted on a summer's afternoon rather than at dawn as usual, because surveillance had shown that the targets were more likely to be in then. Information on the home dog was non-existent this time, except that there was one, and so PC Sleightholm was instructed to get himself up to the dog school to draw one of the new protective suits from stores.

Cass occupied one half of the van. The suit filled the other half. Back at the station, Joe unloaded the gear into an interview room and went through it, concluding immediately that he wasn't going to manage the fitting on his own. Volunteers to help him, including two WPCs, formed an orderly queue. Those who couldn't get in the interview room watched through the one-way window.

The boots were almost knee-high, made of extremely stout leather, seemingly of the sort used to make cricket and hockey balls, and had steel toe-caps. The trousers were hessian, woven from jute, a very strong, woody fibre traditionally employed for sacking but which in more modern times has found uses in, for example, motor-car manufacture and landscape gardening. The jute used in Joe's suit trousers was made into cloth about an inch thick. The resultant garment needed to be supported by leather braces that could otherwise have done duty holding down the bonnet of a Bentley Speed Six. The jacket was made of the same material and had another mighty leather strap fastening under the crotch.

Such an outfit seemed to have been designed to repel RAF bullets as well as their dogs, which was just as well since the wearer would have been unable to do any dodging or leaping for cover. There were various comments from the spectators about Sir Lancelot and needing a winch to lift Joe onto his horse, which had better be a Suffolk Punch, Clydesdale or similar. Joe pointed out that he would happily swap for a suit of armour, as armour at least had joints in it. As it was, he couldn't bend legs or arms, not so much Sir Lancelot as the Angel of the North in winter plumage. Not that it was winter: it was a hot August afternoon and the motorcycle helmet used to top off the ensemble removed Joe's last possibility of a cooling breeze.

Joe was now impregnable to – but unable to escape from –

attacks by lions and tigers as well as pit-bull terriers, but still the health and safety industry wasn't finished. He had also been issued with an electric cattle prod, to be gripped in his right hand, which was somewhere up there inside the sleeve. The stiffness of the sleeve meant that any animal on the offensive would have to throw itself at the prod, rather than Joe being able to use it in the manner of, say, a fencer with an epée.

As he waddled forth, arguments broke out as to which notable character from the cinema he most nearly resembled. Some favoured Frankenstein's monster, some the Tin Man in *The Wizard of Oz*, some Kenneth More playing Douglas Bader with his two tin legs in *Reach for the Sky*. Kenneth More won the vote, walking on his two tin legs while demonstrating with his arms the wingspan of a Spitfire.

Unable to bend sufficiently to fit into a seat, Joe was loaded into the back of a Transit van as if he were a roll of carpet. Meanwhile, the other officers on the raid maintained a respectful silence. At the address, two PCs went to the door with their 'opener' – the modern ramrod device that had replaced sledgehammers – while two more unloaded Joe and helped him stagger towards the soon-to-be-open doorway. The sound of a dog barking could be heard, but not by Joe in his helmet. The door fell off its hinges. Joe, shoved to the front, could not get through. They turned him sideways and heaved. He shot in like a cork out of a champagne bottle, whereupon the guard dog, a rather fat and elderly Jack Russell, whimpered in fright and ran into the kitchen.

Joe took his helmet off and was rendered speechless by the

sight of 'Mac' McKay and his Springer coming in to search for the drugs. Mac told Joe that the press were outside wanting to interview him. One of his so-called colleagues advised him to keep the suit on because they were going to take him to an unexploded bomb. Another suggested that it was only its newness that made the outfit so stiff and awkward, and if he kept it on for a day or two it would be nice and soft for the next person to have it.

The next person, thought Joe, would not be him – not at any price. He got the suit off in the back of the Transit and waited to be shipped back to the station in his socks and underpants. The first person to say anything would be asked, 'Have you met my dog Cassius?'

* * * * *

A handler and his dog are, obviously, a more expensive resource than a normal PC. The training, allowances for the dog's care, a seven-hour day for the officer – one hour a day spent grooming, exercising, cleaning the kennel – boarding costs for holidays and so on, all added up to a financial argument. Wasting Joe's time in a silly suit was one thing, but another was those quiet periods when jobs strictly for the dogs were not coming up. An accountant at HQ might look at the books and ask how all this money could be justified.

Dog handlers would argue that they were police officers first, like anybody else, and when they weren't specialising they were a general asset to the force, like an extra crime car with a dog in the back. Even so, there were days and nights when the coffee flask was empty long before its time.

On such a night, Cass was asleep in the van and Joe had decided to have his last cup even though his shift had three hours to go, when a message came over on the radio about a spate of phone-box thefts, in a line following the main road from Clufford to the big city. This was the crime of the moment. Somebody had discovered that if you took a cordless drill with a metal-boring bit and made a hole in a certain place in the coin box, you could insert a screwdriver and, with a lift and a push, bring the coin-holding part right out. The word soon went around and, for a while, all the scallywags were at it. There was a belief that if you made a call to the number of the box you were drilling, for example from the next box you were planning to do, the engaged line wouldn't allow the normal alarm to go off at the exchange when you drilled the hole. This didn't actually work, but it didn't normally matter to the thieves because they only did two or three boxes anyway, then disappeared into the night.

The description of a line of half a dozen phone-box alarms, all heading in the same direction, made Joe throw his coffee away – on his offside rear tyre, as he liked to do – and set off for a point of interception, where he sat and waited. Various vehicles went past. Joe was wary. It hadn't been very long since he'd pulled over an estate car full of all kinds of junk at two in the morning, only to find that the driver was a professional one-man band returning from a distant gig.

A nondescript saloon came along with four men in it. Joe

pulled out and followed. Cass snoozed on. A check on the national computer revealed nothing of use. There was a T-junction up ahead. If the car turned left towards the big city, Joe would stop it. If it turned right towards the coast, he would let it go. It turned left.

The four men in the car were quite mature and just a touch menacing: powerful physical specimens, if probably retired from the main fray. The front-seat passenger had a well-worn leather hold-all at his feet. Joe gave it a prod and a rattle. It was full of tools, including several drills. Another prod was enough to tell him what that the canvas bag next to it was full of coins.

Four men – clearly characters to be reckoned with – Joe, and his dog: that was the balance of things. Cursing himself for not opening up the van so Cass could be whistled up to take part in this, he asked the driver to step from the car as he needed to give him a producer, that is, a ticket to produce his documents at the station within five days. Walking as quickly as he could without hurrying, Joe went to his van, opened the dog cage, pressed the emergency button and called for back-up. As he did so he heard footsteps – running, receding – and the sound of car doors opening, quickly followed by the sound of doors closing as Cass rocketed up to the car and stood guard.

The next sound was the distant but welcome one of a police siren. The runner would have to be left to run until this help arrived, which was only a few minutes but seemed an age to Joe. The two bobbies in the horn-playing section car took over custody from Cass of the three villains and called for more help. Now the problem Joe had was one of borders. They were right on the boundary line with the neighbouring force. Strictly speaking, he should call control and ask them to ask the neighbours to send a dog handler, by which time all would be lost.

He didn't spend any time on the harness either. This would have to be free tracking, which was frowned on in some circles but mainly because some dogs responded to freedom by disappearing. Cass wouldn't do that. Neither did Joe bother with the challenge except as a trigger for the dog. No point in shouting.

Police-force borders meant nothing to Cass and he was on to the track right away, which was reassuring because there would be flak from the inspector if Joe's trespass led to nothing. The fugitive had run down an alleyway between houses and open country, jumped a five-bar gate into a field that had been recently sown, and headed across and away. After almost two weeks without rain, the going was good and the man had put a fair distance between himself and his pursuers.

This didn't bother Joe yet. He had faith in Sleightholm's Law: that a villain will keep going when pursued by a member of the public but will stop and hide from the police. Such a villain would not know he had Cass on his tail, and Cass needed no encouragement. He was ripping along and Joe was having difficulty keeping up. They came to a farmyard, concrete, much more of a problem to track on, and Cass seemed confused. There were several farm buildings, ancient and modern, and the dog ran around them all without any kind of a signal that he'd found. Joe sent him around again and this time there seemed to be a slight preference for one of the barns. Perhaps the coin thief had tried all the outbuildings and chosen this one.

Cautiously, Joe opened the door. Cass was in, scurrying about, finding the scent, confirming it, but not able to work out such a puzzle in pieces, until he stopped and stared upwards. No, that couldn't be it, so off he went again, but again he stopped and looked up. Had he heard a tiny sound? Joe shone his torch into the rafters, just in time to see a foot being withdrawn from sight.

With Joe's assurances that Cass was a well-behaved animal and entirely under control, the man was persuaded that the adventure was over. He climbed down. Cass did a stand-and-speak just to make sure that their agreement was solid, and the man held out his hands for the cuffs. 'How did you know which car to stop?' he said.

'I didn't,' said Joe. 'The dog told me.'

* * * * *

When Dr Beeching closed all those railway lines, he had no notion of the amount of long-distance footpaths he was donating to the nation; nor, indeed, of the escape routes he was providing for juvenile car thieves. Four of these, all with matching baseball caps, after being chased by traffic police through the highways and byways, drove into a lamp-post. They abandoned their joy ride and ran for it. The bobbies chased but lost them, somewhere along a disused railway line, now renamed the Cordwanglers' Way or some such. Joe had been listening to the car chase and wasn't at all surprised to get the call.

A row of modern houses with long gardens backed onto the old line at this point. Joe thought that the gardens might provide fruit. Cass seemed to think so too, because he showed a lot of interest in a shed at the bottom of one of the gardens, close up to the fence dividing it from the old line. Joe came up to consult but was not impressed. He could hear what was inside the shed: pigeons, cooing. Telling Cass that there was work to do and no time to waste on birds, he sent the dog searching further down the line. Three or four houses along, Cass leaped over the fence and, with a triumphant growl, grabbed something. Whatever it was it didn't make any noise. By the time Joe got there it was in shreds. It had been a cheap, imitation leather jacket, probably nicked from a market stall, certainly discarded by one of the thieves, and possibly he wasn't too far away.

Instead of following this up, Cass ran back to the pigeon loft. Before Joe could stop him he was over the fence and trying to get underneath the shed. Joe called him various names but Cass took no notice. There was something nasty in, or under, the woodshed. Sighing with resigned frustration, Joe clambered over the fence and shone his torch under the shed. There he beheld a symphony in pink, a shell-suited teenage boy, a spotty youth of the type that cannot resist the urge to steal a car and drive it into a ditch or, in this case, a concrete lamp standard.

'Down, Cass,' said Joe. 'Come on out, son. Come on. I won't bite you. He might, if you don't come out. Now.'

The boy responded and slid out from under. He was a wiry little sod. He sold Joe a dummy with a sidestep that any rugby winger would have been proud of and was over the fence in a twinkle – unfortunately for him, right into the arms of the two traffic cops who were puffing onto the scene. The momentum of the fleeing boy took all three of them down in a tussling heap of arms and legs.

Joe sensed a black-and-brown flash go past him, saw his magnificent Cassius take the fence without touching, and watched as he buried his teeth into a pink leg. The tangle of bodies quickly resolved itself into two laughing policemen and a very quiet boy who, after his initial yell of agony, had decided he was a man and wasn't going to show any signs of pain or distress. The cops took him to the station while Joe and Cass continued the search. This may have been the operationally correct choice but, in the modern police force, a biting requires a written report, and a bureaucratically minded senior officer might have thought that the report should come first.

In fact it was a thus-minded custody sergeant who called Joe in, away from his man-hunt, and Joe was not pleased. He threw open the door at the station and looked daggers at the sergeant.

'Do you know your dog's bitten the prisoner?' said Sarge. The reply was obvious but, in the circumstances, inadvisable.

'No,' said Joe, 'but if you hum it I'll try and sing along.'

'Don't get funny with me, son, or you'll be in for disciplinary action.'

Joe asked to see the prisoner, and asked the prisoner to see his bite. He pulled down his pink pants and showed Joe four deep punctures in his thigh.

'God, you're going to be sore in the morning,' said Joe. 'Are you going to make a complaint?'

'Occupational hazard, mate,' said the lad. 'Some dog you got there. Bit me like that and never did nothing to my kecks. Look.

Not a mark. If he had, I would have complained. Cost me a fortune, this suit. Never nicked it. Had to buy it in a shop.'

* * * * *

The clocks had gone back, so an earlier nightfall meant shorter hours for the local burgling community, most members of which prefer to do their housebreaking in the daytime. The house owners are thus out at their employment, shopping or lunch, rather than asleep in their beds and liable to wake up, and there's no need for lights to alert neighbours. To offset this reduced opportunity for dishonest toil, two of that trade had had a look around an old village pub that, despite being close beside a railway station on a branch line, was called The Mason's Arms. It was there long before there were any pubs called The Railway Tavern or The Station Hotel, which was why the toilets and the kitchen were in a flat roof extension and not an integral part of the design. An agile person could leap from the station platform onto the flat roof and, crouching in the shadows to avoid being seen from below, could force a rickety sash window at first-floor level in the original pub wall and climb in.

There were few people on the train that dark evening, which could have worried the burglars slightly in that someone might have noticed them, but they were confident of carrying off the job and being able to catch the next train back to town. Any noise they might make would never be heard above the thrum and hubbub of two popular bars and a restaurant, and staff would be thoroughly occupied, rushing about serving.

The sash window didn't need forcing. It opened easily and the two burglars switched on the first light they found, a bedside lamp. They were in a plush and luxurious bedroom with plenty of money spent on silks and satins, not necessarily in the best possible taste, but that did not concern the thieves. Their interest lay in the vast dressing table, button-upholstered in a vivid shade of puce as if suitable for an especially self-important soap-opera star. This must have been home to a well-stocked jewellery box. There were several other promising signs, including a locked attaché case, and the burglars were about to start their collection when they heard someone coming up the stairs.

It was half-past nine and the landlady always took a ten-minute break, for a smoke and a cup of tea, before the busy run-in to closing time. The two men were out of the window and gone as the landlady opened her bedroom door. Funny, she thought, didn't think I'd left the light on. And the window. What's it doing open?

Dashing across the room and peering out into the darkness, she thought she saw something, or someone, and she certainly heard a crash and a grunt of pain as whatever she'd seen fell over some beer crates. Pausing only to make sure the attaché case was still there, she rang 999 from her bedroom phone. She was told not to touch anything and she didn't, except for stashing the attaché case under the old jumpers in the bottom wardrobe drawer.

PC Sleightholm was some miles from the pub but he acknowledged the call, 'Intruders disturbed', and put in a request for any local officers arriving before him not to try searching the countryside. Leave it to the dog. He switched on his blue light and horns and accelerated away. This would have been the signal for some dogs to bay like a wolf and scrabble at the van doors to be out. Not Cass. He went back to sleep. When the van slowed down and stopped, that would be the time to get excited. He'd been in the force almost a year now. He knew what was what, on the street and off it.

When Joe got there, the only police presence was one DC on the blower to Scenes of Crime. Cass went into harness and they began looking. The dog displayed no interest in anything around the pub so they went over to the station, both platforms well lit and bare, and still nothing to be scented. Back at the pub, the DC made some smart-arse remark about dog food being expensive these days. Joe thought the crooks had probably come and gone in a car but the DC said the landlady hadn't heard a car. She seemed to think they'd legged it.

All right, then. We'll let the dog sort it out. Joe let Cass go with a 'Where is he?' and followed. At first Cass went around the pub yard, where he'd already been, though he was more interested this time and almost casually took a line away from the railway, down a lane, and into a field maybe 150 yards away. It was newly ploughed. Perhaps the farmer was planning on drilling it with winter barley.

Cass kept searching, but there were no indications that he'd found a track. Then he did a very strange thing. Nose down, he made a circle in the middle of the field, a wide circle, 150 yards across, then another, smaller one, and so on, ever decreasing in a spiral, in silence. He'd been around half a dozen times before he stopped and put his head down and began eating something. Sod it, thought Joe, he's found a bloody hedgehog. All this carry-on and it's a dead bloody hedgehog.

But no, it was something else, something without sharp prickles. Cass was biting into it, and ripping it up and shaking his head. A pheasant? Was he plucking a pheasant? Joe's stroll over the field, to give Cass a telling-off, turned into a canter as a plaintive moan issued from the pheasant, followed by a shout of pain and a 'Gerroff you ****ing bastard, that's my best jacket.'

Joe arrested and cuffed the burglar, who'd been left behind by his mate after spraining his ankle jumping off the flat roof and landing in a pile of beer crates, and advised him to wear something other than a real-leather jacket on future jobs. 'He likes leather, you see, does my dog. Try tweed. Or vinyl. Interesting how he found you, wasn't it, going round and round in circles. And he didn't bark. Very odd. He's never done that before.'

CHAPTER NINE

THE MAN HE SHOULD HAVE AVOIDED

Advanced training would seal the partnership. The handler and the dog, now with a year's experience, would go back to school for a fortnight and graduate from advanced training as the finished article, the complete unit. There would always be refresher days too, and opportunities to try things out, but a police officer and dog who got through those two courses and came out with approval from the instructors would have to be as equipped for the job as well as anyone in the world could be.

The bones of the course were: tracking in extra-difficult circumstances, such as on a hot, sunny day on a hard surface; irretrievable article, something too big and/or heavy for the dog to retrieve, so what does he do; send away and redirect, giving the dog lines to explore by word and gesture, at a distance of up to one hundred yards; and complex scenarios in buildings with multiple criminals.

Hard-surface tracking is difficult because there is so little for the scent to stick to. Criminals tend to make it easier by running in straight lines, so a good way to ease into it in training is to start the track on grass and move on to a hard surface, which was why they went to a World War Two aerodrome. Biro ran across the rough stuff, then pelted up the runway while the class was having a brew around the big van.

'Right,' he said when he came back. 'It'll get no better than this. Overcast, no wind and a fresh track. Joe, you go and start, up there about two hundred yards. Dave, you go and lay one. Down there, grass about a hundred yards; tarmac, five hundred.'

The difference between grass tracking and aerodrome-runway tracking became glaringly obvious immediately. Cass slowed right down, from a swift gallop to a funeral march, and began checking his work, making sure of what his nose was telling him before moving on. A track in long, wet grass was a continuous stream of information in full flow. On dry tarmac, it was a series of tiny mysteries of varying quality, with gaps between. Someone running could leave very big gaps, and for the dog to approve of these disjointed, widely separated, inconsiderable bits of mixed data as a track, there were decisions to be made that could not be rushed. Would the faintest whiff of a footprint, followed by nothing, imply another faint footprint or not? Would there be enough carry in the smell that shouldn't be there to keep the dog interested? Had the dog the ability to concentrate? Had he the clarity of mind to keep at it long enough and hard enough?

At first, it seemed to Joe that Cass wasn't doing it. There was a superficial aimlessness about it, but Biro was right behind, whispering, telling Joe what was happening and constantly exhorting him to have faith. It was difficult, when all the handler could see was a perfectly blank runway and all the dog could smell was the equivalent of primitive shortwave radio on a very bad day for reception. The signal came and went, always with background interference but, if you believed, you would eventually get the message.

It would be almost two years before this training came into full use for Joe and Cass and a very full use it was. Two men described as wearing prison blue were reported mooching around a motorway service station. When a police car arrived, the two men were seen scurrying off into the undergrowth. With Joe on the way and pleading with the bobbies not to try and follow, the track was fresh and the point of entry known. Through the long grass they went, Cass straining on his harness as usual, inhaling the smell that shouldn't be there and disregarding obstacles that might cause Joe to cut his shins, or trip over, or lose his hat to a briar. These were not Cass's problems. He was on the scent.

This was great. There was agricultural land, then a lane that they went straight across, then more fields, and then a theme park. It was ten o'clock at night. The place had been full of people all day and the first obstacle to cross was the acres of concrete they'd been parking their cars on. Cass slowed but didn't hesitate. It would have been impossible to find the track had they not been introduced to it on the spot, and it was a brilliant feat to keep to it all the way over this expanse of unforgiving territory stinking of oil and rubber, but the boys in prison blue were not so far ahead. Cass could still get it.

Another lane, and a farm track – not so difficult with loose material to hold the scent – then a farmyard. They'd been going for an hour and a half, with Joe giving a commentary on his radio. Back at HQ they were following the track on a map and it was heading for a river with a quiet lane running beside it. Surely the fugitives would go left or right, and not across where there was no bridge? Two section cars were dispatched to sit beside the lane at either end, with no lights on, and one soon had the escapers. They were exhausted anyway and gave no trouble, even though they must have known they'd be going back to a harsher regime than the one they'd run away from. Cass and Joe continued the track until they reached the pick-up point, more to see if they could do it than for any legal reason. Had the two runners been fleeing car thieves, the track would have been evidence to link them to the car, almost two hours' march further back, although whether Cass's nose would be sufficient to defeat a clever defence counsel was another matter.

There were two sorts of irretrievable articles. There was the one out of reach that the dog could see and could have retrieved if only he could have got at it, and there was the one in reach but too big, awkward and/or heavy to be retrieved. Both sorts needed to have fresh human scent, or not to have been there long enough to have taken on the smells of the immediate environs.

Joe began with an old anorak, much used on long walks in the Lake District and heavily perfumed with Joe and The Golden Rule in Ambleside, The Dog and Gun in Keswick, The Wasdale Head and the many other pubs he'd been in while wearing it. He hung it securely on a tree branch, in sight but out of reach, went back the hundred yards or so to where Cass was waiting impatiently and sent him off with a 'Find.' Joe followed closely. He needed to see what Cass would do when he caught wind of the anorak, what sort of a sign he would give to show that he'd found.

Most dogs will chase a squirrel and, mostly, they will learn that once the squirrel gains a tree it's gone. There is no point in worrying further. This realisation alone will never stop a dog trying to catch a squirrel, but it may well prove to the dog how pointless it is to wait under the tree, barking.

To wait under a tree barking is precisely what a police dog must do. While the private dog owner, embarrassed at his squirrel chaser in the park, may give a rebuke, the police handler will encourage and praise. Cass, like any other first timer at irretrievable articles, was trying to work out how he could get that anorak. He ran around the tree, put his front paws on the trunk, ran around again, while Joe kept telling him to find – 'Come on Cass, find it, come on, watch him, where is it, Cass you great useless lump' – until in sheer frustration the dog sat, stared at the anorak, and barked at it.

Objective achieved, lots of praise and ear rubbing and let's do it again. With Cass certainly, and most of the dogs usually, finding the object was not the problem. The art of it was getting them to tell the handler where the object was.

The object normally used for physically irretrievable was an old portable safe. Portable, that is, on a builder's wheelbarrow. Again, Cass did what they all did. He tried to get a hold on it, he scratched at it, he ran around it. He wanted to take it back to Joe and he didn't understand why he couldn't do that simple thing. Eventually, frustration and irritation combined and he barked at it.

Job almost done – almost, because there was a further sophistication to consider. Suppose the object were not as formidable as a safe? It could still ultimately be irretrievable, but not so obviously that the dog wouldn't keep trying. Operationally, if you were looking for any large object, whether it was a body in a sack, a bag of tools or a bicycle, you wanted the dog to give notice on finding, not after twenty fruitless minutes trying to drag it out of the bushes. The object they used for this was the wheel and tyre from a small car. When first tried, it had been an inflated one, but a dog accidentally got it upright and bowled it along, creating an entirely new game of 'chase the car wheel'. Since then, it had always been a flat tyre.

Sending away and directing at a distance are probably two of the hardest things to achieve and some operational dogs never do get the hang of it. On their initial training course, handler and dog had stayed close, mostly, and mostly the exercises ended with getting the dog to come back. Here they were doing exactly the opposite and even Cass got confused.

Biro told Joe what to do and sent him off to a football field to do it. This was one exercise where there should be no distractions from other dogs and men. Joe sat Cass down on the centre circle. Cass watched, tail going again for a new game, as Joe walked towards one of the goals, turned on the penalty spot and walked back again. Nothing very interesting so far, until Joe crouched down next to the dog, left arm around him, pointed with his right to where he'd just been, let go and said, 'Away.'

Cass got up, didn't bother with the track and ran, out of curiosity more than anything. As he reached the edge of the penalty area, Joe shouted, 'Down.' By the time the sound had travelled and Cass had registered the call, he'd be on the penalty spot. And so he was, except he didn't go down. He was looking for some other reason for being there.

'Down,' called Joe. 'Down, Cass.' Well, all right, he did know what 'down' meant, and Joe speed-walked towards him and made a big fuss. Together they walked back to the centre spot, faced the other goal and did the same again. This time, Cass dropped on the first command. They did it on all four corner flags, then went to a goal mouth and did it for the centre spot. This was really not a problem to Cass at all and so, rather than overdo it, Joe decided to try the progression.

They went to the centre spot. Cass sat. Joe didn't go anywhere, but crouched and said, 'Away.' Cass stared at him blankly. He was changing the rules again. No sooner did a dog learn a game than the gamesman did something silly. 'Cass, away, away,' said Joe in his best commanding tone – and well I never, the dog got up and did it. What a fuss was made and what praise lavished. Cass was thoroughly delighted, although for what reason he hadn't yet quite understood, but a short refresher the next day firmly implanted the exercise.

Once that was sorted, Cass had to move on to the real reason for doing it. He had to learn to search under direction from a master who could not be with him, for one reason or another. Operationally it was unlikely to happen. It was one of those elements of training in which difficulty and potential usefulness were not balanced. Cass's present difficulty was to learn the difference between right and left.

This is something that many humans are unable to fathom as long as they live, especially when reading a map. Cass usually had his own map-reading instrument, his nose, which would be no help to him now.

'Down, Cass,' said Joe, and walked 20 yards to one side, where he stuck in the ground a small, white-painted, rusting metal flag that at some point had marked a cricket field boundary but was now in work as a direction-finding beacon. Cass watched, expecting a new game, tail swishing in the grass.

Joe walked on a diagonal away from the flag and the dog, until he was 20 yards from Cass and directly in front. He faced the dog, who looked at him with interest. Putting as much showbiz as he could into his gesture, Joe waved his left arm in a grand half-circle, pointed left, and called, 'Cass, go left.' To Cass, of course, it wasn't left at all. It was stage right. Not that it mattered, because the dog got up, had a little sniff at a very elementary track then didn't bother, cantered to the little flag, pulled it out of the ground and took it to Joe. He sat in front of his best friend with the flag crossways in his mouth, didn't drop it because he knew Joe didn't like that, and looked terribly pleased with himself.

Joe, so wrapped up in willing his dog on, had forgotten to say, 'Down' when Cass reached the flag. 'I'm a pillock,' he told Cass. 'Prat of the first water. Now, if you would be willing to accompany such a lame-brained wazzock, we'll do it properly this time. Leave. Good lad.'

He sat Cass down again, walked in the same direction as before but another five yards extra, planted the flag, returned to his observation spot and did his grand gesture. 'Left, Cass, go left,' he called, and 'Down' with an extra sharpness when the dog reached the flag. Cass, unsure and confused, barked at the flag. It was obviously the object at the bottom of this particular mystery, the fly in Cass's ointment, so he gave it a good barking then lay down and stared at it.

'Nearly spot on, Cass,' said Joe, and seven repeats later it was so spot on he could do it without the flag. Ten similar runs but going right, and Cass could do that too. The question was, if ordered one way or the other without the flag and without the precedent of going to the flag, would he be able to choose correctly? Would he go at all? They walked off to a different part of the grounds, and tried it. The answer, to start with at any rate, was no. He ran around in a circle, he barked, he went off searching for his little white flag, he did everything but.

Joe tried it again with the flag. No problem at all. Cass would go as many times as Joe might want to the flag, and follow that again without the flag in the same direction. Cass could go either way without the flag, provided it was the same direction the flag had just been in. What he could not do was hold both ideas in his mind at the same time and choose between them, even with Joe's theatrical gestures. But it would come, Joe was sure. It just needed more practice, and then more practice after that.

Operational dogs very often experienced failure. A track would lead nowhere, a search would find nothing, a quarry pursued would escape, and no matter how much the handler tried to compensate with fun exercises out of hours, any failure left a small mark and repeated failures accumulated. Success at new challenges, new games, was an unbeatable tonic for a dog and handler.

'Multiple persons', in which toilets usually featured strongly, was always a good one. People on the run in a building often headed for the loo, with the idea of locking themselves in a trap and standing on the seat, or maybe climbing out through a small window. Such things, the course was assured, did happen in reality as well as in TV cop shows, and Biro asked each handler to take a turn in devising an exercise. Bobbies being bobbies, this was a chance to expose a colleague to maximum embarrassment, but that had to be done without affecting the dog in any negative way.

They were on a day out, standing together in the reception hall in the main block of a disused holiday camp. The chalets were long gone, replaced by another set of boxes made of bricks and arranged in rows of avenues and closes, while arguments continued to rage in high places about what to do with this building, a fine example of late art deco, having been built soon after the war to a design very reminiscent of the Midland Hotel at Morecambe. The arguments meant that the police had been able to use it for several years and the more experienced dog handlers had become quite familiar with it, and, of course, the toilets which, as one would expect for 1940s building standards, were solid rather than fancy, ideal for police-dog training.

Joe had been here with his previous dog and he volunteered to go first. He'd thought of an idea the night before, which was why he was wearing an elderly tweed sports jacket, demoted several times from 'smart', through 'pub', through 'all right for dog walking', to 'gardening only'. He tied Cass to a radiator and walked briskly down a corridor, through a great room that was once the dining hall, down another corridor and into the gents. He folded his aromatic jacket and placed it on the closed seat of a WC, the middle one of five, and shut the door on himself without locking it. He climbed over the partition into the next compartment, and the next, and out of that one to stand in front of the obligatory window. It was not a very large window but he could get through using various techniques he had learned from housebreakers over the years.

By now, someone (one of the newer boys, he hoped) would have set a dog away to find him. He slid around the side of the building, waited in the main entrance until the dog barked and everyone rushed off, and ran after them. In the gents was the familiar scene. The dog was sitting in front of the WC door, barking his head off. The handler, charged up with his success and wanting to charge the dog up even more, was calling, 'Come in number seven, your time's up.' Everyone else was watching. On operations, the handler might say, 'Come on out, you little shithouse.' In training, with his man found, he screamed at the top of his voice, 'What are you doing in bed with the coalman, darling? It's the milkman we owe money to,' then, 'Come out, and bring your filthy magazine with you' in a tone that made it clear that this was Joe's last chance to get out alive.

Joe, standing behind him, tapped him on the shoulder. 'Send the dog,' he said. 'Honestly, I really don't mind about that jacket.'

He who lives by the joke shall die by the joke. Later in the day came 'multiple criminals', the idea being to make the dog understand that his job was not necessarily finished when he found and detained his first man. The standard procedure was to have one criminal in the open and one elsewhere, hidden. The dog would quickly find the open one, detain him until he was escorted away, and be set off to look for the second.

Glen was arranging this one, for Joe and Cass. He put the young handler who'd been taken for a ride by Joe inside the same WC cubicle with the door bolted, crouching on the seat, with a book to read, while he stood himself outside the door. Cass found Glen in seconds, barked, and bounced on his toes. Joe duly arrested him and sent Cass off to search again.

'You stupid animal,' shouted Joe when Cass ran back to the same place and barked. 'You've been there, done that. Cass. Down. Thank you. Now. Where is he?'

Three times he sent Cass off in various directions, and three times the dog came back to the same WC door, to the accompaniment of all sorts of exasperated insults that Cass took calmly. He knew he was right, he knew he'd found, and it was only a matter of time before Joe realised it. When Joe was about to send Cass off for the fourth time, Biro suggested that he remember the golden rule.

'What golden rule?' asked Joe sharply, getting more and more irritated at his dog for showing him up in front of colleagues.

'The golden rule that states: always trust your dog.'

'Down Cass, good boy,' said Joe, as he did a pull-up on the WC door and looked inside, where the young PC smiled up at him and made sure he saw the cover of the book he was studying, which had a picture of a Labrador puppy and the title *Dog Training Secrets*.

Dave Archer's dog Zero was next, the low-slung one, the snake in the grass. The open criminal on this one was a WPC. They always liked to have a WPC on the course because, when she played the criminal role in a chase and attack, it got over the dogs' natural reluctance to bite a woman. She decided to sit in the stalls of the theatre. It was a very nice little theatre, about five hundred seats, with circle and two boxes either side that were sealed off and locked, but all the rest was open, including dressing rooms, backstage storage with stacks of scenery, and a stage adequate for whatever shows they might put on in a holiday camp if not for a full-size production of *42nd Street*.

It had an eerie atmosphere, as such places do that once were filled with music and laughter but have heard nothing for years except the odd mouse scurrying about. Zero had found his open woman sitting in row D with no trouble at all but was taking a long time over his hidden one. Everybody was in the alleyway at the front of the stalls or in the pit where once a band had played, listening, and Dave the handler was getting increasingly worried. A quarter of an hour went by and not a sign of the dog. Biro looked at Dave, Dave looked at Biro. The deep quiet, in that dusty old place never meant for any silence longer than a dramatic pause, made it almost impossible to speak, but Dave had to give in eventually.

'Come,' he called, intending to set Zero off again when he turned up, but instead they all heard a scrabbling noise from above, looked up and watched with sheer horror and disbelief as Zero launched himself from the front row of the circle. He landed in the centre aisle, seemingly on his head, and lay still. Dave was first to him.

'He's still breathing. Call an ambulance.'

'Dave, we can't call an ambulance to a dog,' said Biro.

'Well do some ****ing thing. How did he get up there? Who checked the doors?' Dave raised his face briefly to his friends and fellows, tears streaming down his cheeks, and turned back to Zero, his faithful hound, who had trusted his master so much that he took death's leap without a second's hesitation.

'There's an old rug in the foyer. It'll just do,' said Joe, running off.

'Glen,' said Biro. 'Go and get your van and bring it right up to the front door. I'll radio the school, tell them to organise the vet. We'll take him straight there, to the vet's.'

Joe came back with the rug. They lifted the still-unconscious dog onto it and carried him to the van. Dave wanted to drive, but Joe pushed him out of the way.

'I'm the one who came top,' he said, meaning his marks on the advanced driving course. 'You get in the back with the dog.' With blue light flashing and horns wailing, they broke every standing instruction about speed limits while Biro called all units on the radio telling them to keep out of the way unless they could do something useful. A traffic car pulled out of a lay-by in front of them, also with everything flashing and wailing, and cleared the route.

The vet was ready and waiting, fully briefed on the fall. Zero was beginning to stir and moan so he was given an injection, while the treatment room began to fill with police.

'This is not the Royal Society,' said the vet. 'I'm not doing a demonstration. Next of kin only, please.'

Dave grabbed Joe by the arm as the rest all left. 'Stay with me, brother,' he said.

After a great many mmms and quite a few ahas, the vet pronounced. 'PC Archer, isn't it? Yes, well, you're very lucky, or should I say the dog is. He'll certainly live, he has no internal injuries that I can see, but he's lost some teeth and broken his jaw in two places. If he'd landed in among the seats he would almost certainly have suffered something fatal like a ruptured spleen or a broken spine but, given the importance of jaws to a police dog, I have to say I don't think he'll work again. Sorry.'

Dave Archer had some important thinking to do. He'd grown very fond of his snake in the grass, so his first decision was relatively easy. Zero would become the family pet, as far as a police-trained dog could be a pet, which was the dog's future taken care of, but what about PC Archer, dog handler? Would he be able to go through it all again with another dog?

Biro's advice was yes, don't even think about anything else. It's part of the life cycle. You expect a dog to retire before you do, you expect to train and retrain with maybe three or even four dogs in your career, so are you a dog handler or not?

'You can take the policeman out of the dog handler, but you can't take the dog out of the policeman,' said Dave. 'What are you all laughing at?'

Dave disappeared on leave. Zero would recover but had lost for ever, as the vet had predicted, the ability to bite seriously. Zero's was not the only career to come to an end in that holiday camp. It was the following day and again the danger came from an entirely unexpected quarter.

Part of the instructor's task is to build flexibility into his students' attitude. The dog is trained, the handler is trained, and everything goes like clockwork – and then out on the job something entirely unexpected happens. Different instructors had their own favourite tricks for this. Biro liked to distract the dogs in a surprise move and see how the handler dealt with it. He went to hide in a store cupboard in the massive kitchens, but Cass found him easily. Joe gave the dog all the praise as usual as he was putting him on the lead, but didn't think it had been much of a challenge and said so.

Biro's response was to give Cass a tap with his foot, on his ribcage. It was just a light tap, nothing at all, but Cass whipped round and grabbed Biro by the trouser leg. Joe shouted, 'Leave' and yanked hard on the lead. Cass hadn't let go instantly, so the yank upended Biro, who landed on the tiled floor on his right elbow with the dog on top of him. Joe was laughing.

'Leave, Cass. Good boy. What did you do that for, Biro? Don't tell me. You've never done that before.'

'Spur of the moment, Joe. Expect the unexpected. And it's not funny. I think I've broken my elbow.'

Concern, sympathy and urgent action were nothing like as apparent as they had been for Zero. The lads and their dogs enjoyed their days in places like the holiday camp. They liked setting each other up for more and more complicated scenarios with multiple criminals, and it was hardly lunchtime yet. The show must go on was Biro's policy too.

'Glen,' said Joe, 'do you think the missionary position can be done on just one elbow?'

'I don't know, Joe. We'll have to ask Mrs Biro later. There are other considerations too. Pint lifting.'

'Yes, and fish-and-chip eating. You definitely need both moving joints for fish-and-chip eating.' It was only when Biro's face went a kind of very pale green and he fainted to the floor that it was decided that an ambulance should be called. X-rays showed the bones in pieces and no hope for a normal arm when they mended. A national institution of dog training, with many scars to show for his dedication to the cause, decided that was enough. He only had a few months to his 30 years in the job. Bring on the light duties. Let somebody else do the Egyptian sand dance.

Joe was due home with the advanced course complete and Julia had made a big pan of Bolognese sauce. Spag Bog and a bottle of red wine was their traditional way of reintroducing themselves after a period apart, so some of the sauce would be served that night and some would go in the freezer to make a lasagne later. Holly was there, not doing much, Harriet was busy painting a picture, so Joe took Holly and Cass out for some tree work.

All three of them loved this game, which had a serious purpose. A missing child was a possibility in policing every day and, while distressed parents would mostly imagine the worst, often it was simply a case of a child playing somewhere and forgetting about the time, or wandering too far and getting lost in the woods. Police dogs would not want to bite a child and, as a corollary to that, might not regard a child as anything to do with them. Unsure about what Cass might think, Joe regularly mounted his special Holly-up-a-tree exercise. He'd lie Cass down outside a copse they passed on one of their walks and go in with Holly. He'd lift her into a tree and she'd climb a little higher and hide herself among the foliage while Joe went back to Cass by a circuitous route.

With a very gentle 'Where is he?', Cass would usually make light work of the searching and before long Joe would hear two well-known sounds: Cass barking and Holly shrieking with laughter. Cass would get his reward, his favourite toy thrown from above by the delighted little girl, and they'd do it again.

Such was their occupation on this afternoon, while Mummy was doing the ironing upstairs and younger daughter Harriet, now bored with her painting, decided to help Mummy with the cooking. The pan of Bolognese was cool but still on the stove top. Harriet knew that salt and pepper were essential ingredients of savoury recipes, but the pepper grinder was empty and the salt cellar soon ran out as she gave the sauce extra seasoning. Never mind, there was an almost full drum of Saxa in the cupboard. She thought she'd better not put all of it in. Just half would do, and the drum went back on its shelf.

Harriet also knew that grated cheese was to do with Spaghetti Bolognese, only she couldn't find any cheese. She found the grater all right, but the nearest thing to cheese seemed to be these candles. Oh well. They grated just like cheese. She finished one candle and put the wick in the bin, and was on her fifth candle when Julia discovered her. The little girl looked so pleased at helping Mummy on her own initiative that Julia had no heart for scolding. Instead, reasoning that a little candle wax would do no harm and that best butcher's mince should not be entirely wasted, she divided the Bolognese between two dog bowls, one having rather more than the other, and added some biscuit mixer.

When the rest of the family came home, Joe agreed that a few flakes of wax would be no peril to a digestion as all-embracing as Cass's, and garlic would be good for him. Cass thought it was great, but then he thought all food was great. Leila, a little more discerning, sensed something wrong and left it. Possibly she didn't like basil. After the family had had bacon and eggs for an impromptu evening meal, Joe went to get Cass out of his run.

'Julia,' he said coming back into the house. 'Has anything knocked Cass's bucket over?'

'Not that I know of. You filled it this morning.'

'I was sure I had. But it's empty. Cass must have knocked it over. Anyway.'

So Joe filled Cass's bucket with fresh water and watched in amazement as the dog lapped and lapped until it was almost empty again, and Julia came out into the garden holding a drum of Saxa salt.

'The salt cellar was empty, so I went to fill it. I know I got this salt last week. And it's more than half empty. Joe, Harriet has been cooking more than we thought. I've also found four candlewicks in the bin. You'd better take him for his walk as far away as possible.'

As well as being fussy about her food, Leila didn't seem quite so bossy these days. She still made sure that Cass knew his place and gave her the respect due to a stately and elderly female from a bolshie, uppity young male, but she didn't seem to nag and bully him so much. The times she really sparked were on those rare occasions when she managed to get hold of his favourite toy of the moment. She would stand there with it in her mouth – whatever it happened to be, anything from a squeaky plastic hamburger to the fabled clothes peg – her tail twitching in delight, while Cass stared in dismay and confusion, baffled, baulked and very, very annoyed. There she was with, say, that old plastic brush that used to have a dustpan with it. It was his brush, his toy that he was gradually reducing to molecules, and she'd got it in her mouth, and it was his and he wanted it back.

Robbery with violence was out of the question. Perhaps if he went up to her quietly, he could just grab it from her. Or, maybe… no. Well, he couldn't think of anything else, so he would sidle up, and she would stand there, stock still except for the tail going, as if she didn't really care about his horrible old chewed-up brush. Cass didn't understand about pretending not to care. He did care, very much indeed, and it was his brush, and he wanted it, and he would stand close to Leila until he could bear it no longer and he had to make his move… NOW! He would almost get his teeth on it but she had this knack of snatching her head to one side at the absolute last fraction of a second and he would miss. She would move a few paces away, lie down with the brush between her front paws, and have a little nibble at it. Not too much. Just enough to send Cass into a turmoil of frustration. He would make a dash. She would pick up, stand and turn the other way, and Cass could bark and whine as much as he liked. He wasn't going to win.

At least, that was how it used to be. The only way Cass ever got his toy back would be when Joe or Julia retrieved it out of Leila's kennel. Now Leila tired of the game after a while, let the thing go and wandered off. Cass was pleased to get his toy but it was an empty victory somehow, as it always is if a better player lets you win because he can't be bothered to beat you.

Leila was becoming rather deaf, too, and it wasn't the normal dog's selective deafness. This was general deafness. And when they went for walks, she would start off as ever but after half a mile she'd sit down. She didn't want to go any further. They stopped taking her and the awful thing was, she didn't mind. She'd have gone mad before, if she'd seen the family kitting up for a walk and leaving her behind. Now she watched them go and retired to the comfort of her kennel.

When the cold weather came she clearly felt it and they had to bring her indoors. This was another thing Cass couldn't understand. He knew very well he wasn't allowed in the house, and Leila never used to be. So now, if Cass was free in the garden and the back door happened to be open, he would lie with his nose and his front paws over the threshold. If a dog can be jealous, he was.

It became more and more difficult to get Leila to eat anything. Even that dish irresistible to any dog in any state of health, the kipper, was rejected by Leila, interested only in the nice, comfortable bed with patchwork quilt bought by Julia from, respectively, the pet stall on the market and the charity shop.

With Joe away on a course, luckily it was Julia who found her and not one of the girls. Leila, dear old Leila, was stretched out by the back door when Julia came downstairs one morning, as if she'd been trying to get to her kennel, to get home, for her last moments. At first Julia thought she was dead and knelt beside her, tears falling but, as she stroked the dog's ears, there was a flicker of life. Leila's eyes seemed to focus on something in front and her head came up. Satisfied, she rested her head on Julia's lap, opened her mouth slightly as if to give a lick but breathed her last breath.

Julia heard the girls moving about upstairs getting ready for school. She'd never tried to lift Leila before, not an especially large example of the GSD bitch but still probably more than 50 lb, or 20 kg. Eyes full of tears, Julia straddled the corpse, put her arms around Leila's upper body, behind the front legs, and half carried, half dragged her out of the back door, across the lawn and into her kennel. She hoped that the girls would be too busy arguing about whose school tie was whose to look out of the window and see their mother struggling with a dead dog.

If they noticed at breakfast, Julia would say she was in her kennel. By the time they came home from school, the body would be gone and they could have things explained. Leila dead was not the mental picture Julia wanted her daughters to keep. Leila living, on walks, chasing balls, bounding up hillsides – that was the picture they should have.

CHAPTER TEN

THE POLICE DOG IN THE SKY

When helicopters were first introduced to police forces, their more enthusiastic proponents suggested that there was now little need for dogs in their conventional role of finding-and-holding. The magic 'eye in the sky', infinitely more mobile, had high-tech heat-seeking kit to replace the dog's nose, and spotlights, loud hailers and the noise of its rotors to replace the bark. With its panoramic view it would be a far better platform for guiding in reinforcements than a dog handler standing alone in a wood so, apart from drug and bomb sniffing, what need was there for Fido and Rover?

Dog handlers knew that this was a view shared by some senior officers. At the very least, handlers could see their workload being reduced as the glory boys gave priority to the more glamorous helicopter. This was evidence of the effectiveness of modern policing. The public could see and hear it going on. All that chasing across fields in the dark, like a gypsy with a lurcher

– why, that was ancient history. Men had hunted with dogs since Fred Flintstone was a lad. Today's police force was a touch more sophisticated than that.

High expectations percolated down to police control rooms, where the inclination was always to call in the helicopter, except when it was foggy, or there was a gale blowing, or it had developed a technical fault, or it was away doing something else.

Of course, dog handlers and helicopter cops mostly recognised that neither was perfect and neither could do everything. The real improvement in police work would come if they worked together. They knew that, but did the silver-braided ones know that?

Two villages, originally separate but now joined together by development, had gradually become the residential area of choice for the better heeled. Mock-Tudor detacheds with large gardens, built between the wars, alternated with neo-Georgians, 1950s villas, 1960s brutalist machines for living, right up to brand-new infill in solar-panelled splendour. Trees sheltered them all from the glare of hoi polloi going past in buses, and their gravel drives all had the latest model BMWs, Audis and Range Rovers parked on them.

It was these vehicles that sparked an idea in the minds of a couple of city-based burglars. Their usual routine was to turn up at these sorts of houses during the day, in a white van. They would ring the doorbell and if anyone answered they would offer to paint and decorate, re-felt the roof or relay the drive with ornamental brickwork. If no one answered they would break in and steal the jewellery. This was their speciality. Like most burglars, they had their favourite fences who also specialised. Some burglars liked jewellery because they knew where to get rid of it; some did credit cards and passports for the same reason; some did televisions, stereos, computers; and so it went on, each to his own trade.

Our two decided to change tack one day when they spotted a set of car keys on the kitchen table after they'd selected a very fine garnet necklace and other trinkets from the bedroom. The car in question, a showroom-fresh Cherokee jeep, was there, sitting outside the front door. They knew a man who knew a man who exported high-end motors, so the jeep followed the van back to the city.

There were major problems with a plan to break into houses to steal car keys. If the car was in the drive, unlike this first Cherokee occasion, it usually meant someone was at home. If it was a two-car family, the better vehicle was probably in use during the day. So, the work would be better done at night. It was high risk, but the rewards would be known in advance. Instead of hoping there would be some nice bangles and brooches left lying about, they could walk up the street and decide which car they would come back for. If there did happen to be baubles and beads, they could lift them while they were about it.

Another flaw in the plan was the stretch of open country, about five miles of it, to drive through from the pair of villages to the relative safety of the Clufford outskirts, and this presented the police with their opportunity once it became clear to them that the car thefts, a sudden rash of them, were linked. Four vehicles were assigned to the job: a traffic car, in case of a pursuit; two section cars, to stop any suspicious traffic; and PC Sleightholm and Cass in their van in the event of an escape on foot.

The burglars had not offered the police anything in the way of regular behaviour, so a whole week had been set aside. For the first two nights, nothing happened. Some very valuable cars were stopped and the occupants lightly quizzed. A few of the drivers, who had probably been engaging in activities they'd rather their husbands or wives didn't know about, got irate and made pointed remarks about a police state, but most were quite happy to know that something was being done about the thefts.

Around 4am on the third shift, the traffic car was passed by a latest-model BMW saloon heading for Clufford. Unfortunately, the police were going the other way and didn't get the number, and by the time they'd turned round and chased after it, the BMW had disappeared. Everyone spent the rest of the night looking, but there was no trace. Sure enough, at the briefing the next night there was notice of a burglary featuring the theft of a BMW. This was doubly depressing for the cops: one, because they'd missed a chance to nail the burglars; and two, because they didn't think they'd get another. Cars had not been stolen on successive nights. Once a week seemed to provide a sufficiently good living for the villains, so the police expected two more long, boring nights with nothing to do but stop fancy four-wheel drives piloted by attractive blondes.

Joe parked up in a farm gateway and tried to keep himself awake with coffee. Cass was sound asleep in the back. The traffic car turned up soon after 3am and they were having a chat when a new Lexus zoomed past. Pointing the right way this time, the traffic cops said they'd follow and give it a pull, you never know. Joe thought he did know and would finish his coffee.

Two minutes later, a voice came over the radio with that tone that all police recognise: professional, calm, but with an undercurrent of adrenalin. The Lexus had failed to stop. Joe threw the remains of his coffee at his back wheel and joined the queue. He had no chance of catching up with any hot pursuit, not in his 1600 cc van, but he could soon catch up if they stopped and bailed out.

He'd hardly got into fourth before another message came: vehicle abandoned, occupants run off. Minutes later he was there, and so was everybody else, including the sergeant in charge, who was in one of the section cars. They all looked at PC Sleightholm, dog handler, with serious expressions.

'What's up?' he said. 'I couldn't get here any sooner. Do we know which way they went?'

'Have a look in the car, Joe,' said the sergeant. 'Passenger footwell.' Joe looked, and saw a 12-bore shotgun, a box of cartridges and two hand guns. 'The helicopter's not available and the armed response unit is 25 miles away.'

It was a pity about the armed response, thought Joe, as he'd never had the chance to try what they called the diamond formation, which was dog in front tracking in harness, handler behind holding the control line and an armed officer to either side.

'It's up to you, Joe. I can't ask you to do this.' The sergeant looked grim.

'No, you can't,' said Joe, 'but I've got to ask my dog to do it, haven't I?'

'I'll come with you.'

'No thanks, Sarge, you'll put the dog off. Now, if I may suggest...'

They quickly agreed a plan. All units would spread out to the points of the compass to contain the area as best they could, and they'd put in a plea via control for the helicopter from the neighbouring force.

The thieves had a good start, but their most likely route was fairly obvious: through a gate and across the field. The others were getting in their cars, so they didn't see what a mess Joe was making of putting on the harness. His fingers would not perform. Cass was raring to go, and the more raring he was, the more Joe fumbled with his straps. Cass looked back and up at his friend and master. He wasn't usually like this. There was something the matter.

'All right, Cass,' said Joe, 'if you want to know, I'm shitting myself on both our behalves. Right. Got it. Come on. Seek.'

Cass found the track in an instant and was off, leaning into the harness with Joe hanging on. Unlike the instructors setting the tracks followed in training school, which could be anything from a loop-the-loop to a six-pointed star, criminals thankfully tended to think only in terms of the shortest distance between two points. Cass was belting along, but he'd only gone 200 yards when he stopped dead and went down. Beside him was a jacket, a jerkin, with a necklace and some other stuff spilling out of its not-very-deep pockets.

As if they needed confirmation that they were on the trail of the armed villains, this was certainly it. Somewhere ahead of them, still running or more likely hiding, were two men known to carry guns about, and Cass would get to them first. Joe stroked Cass's ears. 'Good lad,' he said, quietly. 'Good lad.' He could barely speak for the lump in his throat. Funny, he thought. I've never done that before.

With another 'Seek on' they were away again, and after another 400 yards came to a wood. Cass wanted to keep going, into the trees, but Joe stopped him. The thieves could only have one purpose in going into this wood. There were no paths, so they must be hiding. If they hoped to get clean away they'd have stayed in the open, where the way was much easier. Joe sat Cass down and hunkered beside him. He tried to shout, 'Come out or I'll send the dog', but all he managed was a croak. Cass looked at him again with that same expression. What's the matter? Why can't I get on with my job?

Harness tracking in rough woodland like this was impossible. The line would get caught in branches and undergrowth. Cass would have to be free, to go it alone. Joe would follow as best he could with his torch, feeling useless and unable to protect his trusting dog from the enemy. He tried again to shout but could not. His mouth was dry and his lungs and tongue would not obey commands. Pull yourself together, Sleightholm. You don't know for sure they've got guns. They could have left them all in the car.

He got on his radio to tell his colleagues where he was and what he was doing, and found himself whispering. Anyway, they heard him all right, and so did Cass, when he whispered, 'Come out or I'll send the dog' in his ear.

Cass knew that such an understated command meant a more measured approach, not to go at it full pelt, and so with Joe following he walked into the wood, nose down. They'd gone maybe 50 yards when Cass seemed to lose the trail and, simultaneously, Joe heard the helicopter. He switched his radio to the dedicated channel. The wood was mainly young birch trees so there was no heavy rooftop canopy of leaves, and it wasn't pouring with rain. With luck the chopper's thermal imaging would work.

'Mike one to dog handler.'

'Yes, receiving.'

'I have hot spots. Can you hold your left arm out at shoulder level.' This would identify Joe from any other hot spots that might be showing on the screen and tell the observer which way he was facing.

'OK, I've got you,' said the man in the air, 'and I've got a spot for the dog.' The spot was the dog's nose, which was all that showed up on those screens. 'And I've got something else. Someone else. He's about ten yards to your left.'

Bleeding bloody hell, thought Joe, as he shone his torch on nothing but trees. 'Dog handler to Mike one. Nobody there,' he said. But, he wondered, had there been somebody there? A man lying on the ground would leave his body heat behind when he moved. The thermal imager would show him as being where he had been, as well as where he now was. But again, if he had been there, surely Cass would have knocked him? Cass was still searching and seemed agitated, like he couldn't finish the puzzle because there was a piece missing.

'No, you're right,' said the airborne one. 'He's about five yards behind you. No, he's not, he's five yards in front. What's wrong with this blasted machine?'

'Stand by a minute, Mike one.' Nothing's wrong with the machine, thought Joe, as Cass stood below a tree close by, looked up and barked. Joe shone his torch into the tree top and saw a young man clinging to it. It was little more than a sapling, a slim silver birch about twenty feet high, and it was bending and swaying with his weight.

'Got one,' said Joe into his radio, his voice back to normal. 'He's up a tree.' Everything was recorded on helicopter jobs, so he switched his radio off for the rest of his speech, which he delivered with dramatic and exaggerated clarity, purely for the benefit of the climbing boy. 'When is the armed response coming in? Or do you want me to move out of the way so you can shoot him from the helicopter?'

There was a rustle and a crack as the young tree gave up its burden. The lad landed in a heap on the forest floor and lay still. Cass stood over him, growling gently. Joe switched his radio to the general channel. 'It's all right,' he said. 'I don't think we've quite got the gunfight at the OK Corral. Forget the cavalry. Forget the heavy mob. Send in the ambulance boys and girls with a stretcher.'

There was much jocularity over the airwaves as tension evaporated. Colleagues came into the wood to remove the felonious youth, who had indeed hurt his leg badly in the fall. When asked where his mate was, he claimed not to have one. He was studying wildlife at the Open University and had come out looking for a badger's nest.

'I didn't know badgers had nests, did you, Joe?' said the sergeant.

'Oh yes, Sarge,' said Joe. 'They build them in rhubarb trees when there's an "R" in the month.'

The helicopter could find no more hot spots and two hours of searching with Cass revealed nothing further. Meanwhile the owner of the Lexus had been woken up and told the story. He had a firearms certificate, was a member of the local shooting club, and he'd gone to bed leaving his guns on the kitchen table where he'd been cleaning them.

This incident, of co-operation between ancient and modern methods of finding an elusive quarry, led to much discussion in high places. There was thinking out of the box, and blue-sky thinking, and running thoughts up flagpoles to see if anyone saluted. There were some good ideas as well: for example, the order came down that dogs were to have familiarisation trips in helicopters. The need had been predicted for dog and handler to be transported rapidly across the division for an urgent search, and that was no time to find out that the dog disliked flying so much that he would bite the pilot.

Another problem raised was the one of the dog van turning up too long after the villains had run off – after a stolen-car chase, say – without helicopter. So, to get there more quickly, a dog and his handler would ride in a traffic car. Cass liked this very much, sitting upright in the middle of the comfortable back seat, lord of all he surveyed. He was certainly lord of the two traffic cops in the front, a male sergeant and a WPC, who already knew about Cass's reputation and never made any unnecessary or sudden movements.

They were heading north on the motorway and it was almost

end of shift when they heard a commentary on a chase, ending in car abandoned, and a call from control asking them to attend as they were the only available dog unit. The blue light went on but Joe told the traffic cops that Cass didn't like the horns. They made him excited. Not true, but it made the traffic cops gulp a bit.

The car, stolen of course, was in the middle of a field with its nose in a ditch. The boy racer in charge hadn't been up to a particular bend, had gone through the hedge and tried to cross what looked like a flattish meadow, not realising there was a drainage channel running through it. The track was fresh and easy and Cass was tracking hard. They came to some heathland. Joe unclipped Cass, called out the challenge and let Cass go. The gorse bushes got denser and denser and bigger and bigger. Cass stopped at the biggest one so far and growled, at the same moment that the helicopter arrived and switched on its spotlight. Joe felt like a character in *Close Encounters* and the dog looked as if he'd bathed in brilliant white emulsion. The police observer in the chopper said there might be someone in the bush but he couldn't tell because the foliage was too dense, and wet from the earlier rain.

Cass could tell, and so could Joe when he shone his torch in. There was your typical joy-riding miscreant, curled up in a ball, pretending to be asleep.

'You've got three choices, son,' said Joe. 'You come out on your own. Or I drag you out. Or the dog drags you out.'

With an elaborate mime of waking up and not understanding what was happening, including yawns, the lad said, 'What's up? Leave me alone. I'm on the Duke of Edinburgh.'

'I'll count to ten,' said Joe.

'I've told you. You're making a mistake. I'm out camping. Turn that light off.'

Joe had lain the dog down about five yards away, concerned that his reputation for biting was growing too much. A successful record of arrests was one thing. A dog out of control was another, which was how some senior officers might see it.

Joe crawled part way into the bush, grabbed a foot and retreated. The boy didn't like it and struggled, again insisting that he was on an outward-bound course and he would ask the Duke himself to complain to the Chief Constable. The lad was face down, kicking and holding on to something with his left hand, a root possibly, while Joe had hold of his left leg. Joe dragged the lad a bit further, but that was it.

Help was at hand. With no other police yet arrived, Cass used his initiative, took off, burrowed into the bush and wrapped his jaws around the nearest limb: the right arm. The car-thief's complaints went up several notches but a three-way tug of war could have only one result. He let go of his anchorage, it became a two-way tug, and a spread-eagled, howling candidate, not so much for gold or silver but more for the Duke of Hazzard rusty tin award, was hauled forth into the spotlight, in front of an admiring audience of two traffic cops who had arrived in time for the show.

The lad was handed over to them, the helicopter could see no more hot spots, Joe and Cass's shift had finished hours ago and so further activity was abandoned. There remained only the issue of how to get home, and Cass was in a pretty state: mud and sand up to the eyeballs.

'Sorry, Sarge,' said Joe to the traffic man. 'You're my dog van at the moment. Your back seat is going to need hoovering.'

'Don't you worry about that, Joe,' said the sergeant. 'I'll hoover it myself. It's been a privilege. Just you make sure he knows who's who on the way home.' He turned to his colleague. 'Heather, take it steady. And for Christ's sake don't turn the horns on.'

That was Cass's last ride in a traffic car. Representatives of the health and safety industry pointed out that if the car were to collide with something hard, a large and hairy missile would be launched from back to front, so variations on the seat-belt theme were experimented with, then a portable pop-up cage. None of them worked, so somebody suggested faster and more powerful dog vans.

Let us suppose, furthermore, said management, that Armed Response have done a hard stop. They surround the car, full of people with guns, and order them all out. The helicopter hovers above, but how do we know that there isn't one still in there, curled up on the back seat or in the boot, with a Kalashnikov? How do we know there isn't a suicide bomber in there, or any other kind of terrorist? The helicopter crew can't see him because thermal imaging doesn't work through a car roof. Can we train a dog to find out?

With great difficulty, thought Joe, and once more we're sending my dog to face dangers that we ourselves are not willing to face. Would it not be better for one of the armed officers to say, 'Come out or I'll shoot'?

Joe pictured the scene. The armed police would spread out

around the vehicle as snipers under cover. He, the dog handler, would have to keep his head down too. Cass, when asked, 'Where is he?', would go straight to one of the police and start barking. If the officer wasn't experienced, he might not stay still and Cass would bite him. Joe got on the phone to Biro.

'I need some help here. You'll have to come out of retirement.'

'Don't be silly. Come round for a beer.'

Biro and Joe developed a plan that required a volunteer to be the baddie. The obvious man to ask was Lanky Laing – PC Nigel Laing, late long ago of the Metropolitan Police, who had transferred to the school a few years before and now was senior instructor in place of Biro. It was standard practice to use instructors for this sort of experimental thing and Lanky, so called because he looked too short to be a copper, would be ideal. He always insisted that he filled the old bill, being five-feet eight-and-a-half inches tall, with good eyesight (with glasses, if worn), nineteen years and over, no offensive tattoos and four O-levels. Nowadays, he would point out, bobbies had never heard of O-levels and a Norwegian troll could join provided he could read and write.

One or two of the instructors were old enough to remember the children's song about Billy Goat Gruff going over the rickety rackety bridge, and the line 'I'm a troll, fol-de-rol, and I'll eat you for supper', and would sing this when Lanky was around and fall about laughing, much to the perplexity of those of the Joe and Glen generation.

The plan was for Lanky to hide on the back seat with the door open, and Joe would give Cass a send-away. When the dog got close enough to the car, Joe would shout, 'Where is he?', thus turning it into a search. Lanky would cheat by giving out the occasional grunt and, if they did it a few times, it might develop into something they could reproduce on operational duty.

Joe, Lanky and Cass met the Armed Response Unit at the dog school. Everyone was very serious and the ARU sergeant gave a short lecture on the importance of the exercise. Joe gave an even shorter lecture.

'This has never been done before, as far as I know. It is new to the dog and new to me. When I first heard about it, I thought it was impossible.'

Joe and Cass went off to get the van while everyone else moved into position. They had to assume that the main phase of the job had been completed. The vehicle had been stopped, the criminals had been persuaded out, made to lie down, been disarmed, cuffed and led away, and it was all over, including the shouting.

Joe and Cass arrived in the dog van, disembarked and took cover behind the engine block. This is ridiculous, thought Joe. I can't direct the dog without watching him, and if I watch him I'm exposed to the hidden gunman. I need a periscope.

Still crouching, he pointed as definitely as he could, arm along the windscreen, looking through the side windows, and said, 'Away.' Cass trundled around the front of the van, had a look and a sniff, and set off to the left for the nearest sniper. 'Down,' said Joe. Cass obliged. 'Go right,' said Joe. This was like telling a starving man that he couldn't have that roast chicken dinner over there, but instead must go in search elsewhere for a beetroot sandwich.

Cass would go right, as ordered, but would then veer towards his chicken dinner. After half a dozen downs and go rights, and with Joe now standing in the open waving his arms about, Cass got near enough to the target car for a loud 'Where is he?', followed by a cough and a throat clearance from Lanky Laing.

Cass was there in two strides and jumped in the back of the car on top of Lanky, who was regretting not dressing up more in, for example, a large and heavy tarpaulin. He needn't have worried. Cass knew Lanky, he was lying very still and so, instead of ripping his best denim shirt to pieces, only growled in a holding kind of way.

The ARU sergeant thought that was it. 'Well done,' he said. 'We'll have to be going. We'll just watch him find somebody in the boot.'

'Hang on,' said Joe. 'We need more practice than that. In the boot? Christ Almighty, what do you want, Mister Ed the Talking Horse?'

'Horse?' said the sergeant.

'All right, you get off,' said Joe. 'I've got the idea. We'll practise on our own and invite you back to the dress rehearsal.'

The exercise went through various stages. Person on back seat with car door open; person on back seat, door closed. Person in open boot; person in closed boot. There were two chief difficulties. One was getting Cass to bark when learning the job with door or boot open. He barked all right with the door or boot closed, but first Joe had to get him to view Lanky in a metal box as more important than another instructor hiding under a bush pretending to be a sniper.

They got it to a fine art eventually and it was incorporated into the syllabus for firearms training. Dog handlers took a pride in being able to do it, but they still thought 'Come out or I'll shoot' was a better idea, and even more so with the next trick Cass was expected to do.

The word came from above, envisaging another scenario that was possible but unlikely to occur often. A mad gunman was holed up in a house. Armed Response had laid siege for hours, but the man wasn't coming out and it was too dangerous to storm the place. Then they heard a shot. Had the man killed himself, or was he laying a trap? How could the truth be known? There could be other situations too, where the need to know what was going on might not justify an officer taking a big risk, but it would be perfectly all right for a dog.

And so Cass was fitted with a video camera. He never did like being laughed at, but there were times when it was hard to stay serious, such as now, when he sat there dressed in the canine equivalent of an Ascot Ladies' Day hat. A flying helmet made out of strong black nylon fabric had had two holes cut in it for his ears and a Velcro strap to go under his chin. The camera, not exactly the latest lightweight model, but one dug out from the bottom of a cupboard somewhere, was fastened to the nylon securely enough, but it still wobbled when the dog moved. 'Heath Robinson is alive and well,' said Joe, 'and working in a police station somewhere in England.' It was an indignity that the dog bore nobly. It was something he had to do, because Joe wanted it.

Joe sat him down outside the house they were using, furnished but currently uninhabited, spoke a few calming words and Cass trotted off in fine style on the command he knew: 'Where is he?' The 'he' in question was a 'she', a WPC who was training for the ARU. She'd been informed beforehand that police dogs didn't bite women. Joe had told her that this was largely true but that Cass was a modern dog with liberal ideas, and he didn't hold with any kind of sexual discrimination. If she lay very still as if dead, everything would be just fine.

She followed Joe's instructions closely, lying in an upstairs room. Joe joined the ARU observer with the TV monitor in a van. The pictures were good and most interesting, seeing things from the dog's point of view, mostly the ground a few inches in front of the dog's nose. Notes were made when Cass gave the camera a thorough rattling, several times, when thrusting his head into spaces that would normally have been adequate but were too small for him in his dog-cam hat.

He didn't waste much time before bounding up the stairs and then, for some reason, turning and running down again. 'I want a copy of that,' said Joe, watching the monitor. 'That is priceless. You could bet anybody a fiver and they'd never guess what it was. Ah, now he's going back upstairs again... into the bedroom... dead body, lie still please. Well done.'

Cass was barking, which again made for some interesting pictures that gave a whole new meaning to camera shake, and so Joe could go in and release the poor animal from his unbecoming headgear.

All these firearms exercises assumed that the ARU would be there, when in reality they often were not. It was more likely, in fact, that an unarmed police officer would come across an armed criminal and have to deal with the situation without help from any specialist quarter. If the officer was a fictitious one in a TV drama, he would walk up to the gunman, palm outstretched and, after a few quiet and persuasive words with appropriate music, the gun would be handed over. Otherwise, not on TV, he would probably call for back-up. But what if he was a dog handler? Could a dog 'arrest' a gunman or suspected gun carrier? Could a dog frighten a gunman into giving himself up?

A procedure was devised. Joe would do the usual 'Stand still or I'll send the dog' routine. The criminal would stand as ordered, Cass would run around behind him and bark and growl and show his teeth, and the criminal would walk forward on Joe's instructions with the dog following as custodian. When near enough, the criminal would be ordered to lie down and Cass would keep guard while Joe searched the man for weapons.

Too hard. Apart from Cass's propensity for biting obedient gunmen in the arse, it didn't seem applicable frequently enough to justify the training. This was another to be passed over to the firearms dog handlers. If they could see a use for it in certain circumstances, maybe they would find the time to work it out properly.

CHAPTER ELEVEN

THE CRY OF HIS HOUND

'Look, officer, I'm sure you're wasting your time. Please don't worry. It's all right.' The old man was so apologetic that Joe was almost persuaded to go. Poor chap, he'd got out of bed after hearing a noise, discovered his back door had been forced, phoned the police, and been quite unable to identify a single item that was missing.

'Thing is, sir, you've been broken into. Even if they didn't steal anything, the fact remains. They could do it again. I'll just put the dog to search your garden. You never know, he might find something they dropped.'

'Oh well,' said the old fellow, 'if you think it'll help. I wish I'd never phoned. All this fuss, and police everywhere. I could have bought a new lock in the morning and not caused any bother. Of course, if my wife had still been alive I would have phoned. She would have made me phone.'

'No bother, sir,' said Joe. 'And besides, it's good practice for the dog.' He went back outside where Cass was waiting, excited because he was at work but patient because he was experienced. 'Cass. Find,' said Joe.

There was some light from the window spilling over the lawn, so Joe didn't need his torch to see what was happening. Cass began as usual with a clockwise circuit, then did his methodical ups and downs. Joe said nothing. No need. They did this at home whenever there were friends round and people wanted a party game. Regulars at Castle Sleightholm were offered a free choice, lucky dip, rummaging inside Joe's Bag of a Thousand Articles – pens, spent cartridges, cigarette lighters, slotted spoons, Dinky toys, Cabbage Patch dolls, clockwork mice, tin openers, kilt pins, even the odd gun or two – but whatever they tried, Cass could never be beaten.

There was a sizeable buddleia in one corner of the old man's garden where Cass twitched, turned and picked something up. He trotted over to Joe, who cupped his hands together in expectation of an offering. Very delicately, because he could be when he wanted, Cass let drop a small, shiny object which, after Joe had polished it in his handkerchief, was revealed to be the body of a ladies' dress watch, quite a nice one, gold with some minuscule stones that sparkled in the dim light and could well have been diamonds. It was tiny, one of those watches worn as decorative jewellery rather than in hope of telling the time, and it had no strap or bracelet. Very good, Cass. Under the heading of 'Articles to be found, small and very small'. Advanced dogs only.

Joe showed it to the man, who burst into tears and sat down

in the armchair. 'It was my wife's,' he said at last. 'How did it get in the garden?'

'No doubt about it, sir,' said Joe. 'The dog picked it up because it had new scent on it, so the burglar must have dropped it. In the morning, have another good check around. Especially jewellery.' The old boy got up and began ferreting in a drawer.

'I will, I will. You see, any jewellery would be my wife's, and I really don't... here. Take this.' He offered Joe a twenty pound note.

Joe, who was feeling the man's distress getting to him and was anxious to be away, said of course he couldn't accept any money, but why didn't sir come to the Children in Need do at the manor house next week? It was only down the road. Cass would be performing in a display, so they could meet up again, and he could put his twenty quid in the collecting tin.

Rehearsing for the display was the only success Cass had for the next few days, until the alarm went off around one in the morning at the region's most prestigious golf club. The waiting list for membership was closed and could only be prised open by the Anglo-Saxon Protestant and/or Masonic nobility, whether ennobled by birth, the honours list, or a plentifully stocked Swiss bank account. The club steward, a retired army captain, was the biggest snob with the least reason to be so, and he was clearly very upset by the burglary, or at least by the thought of one of the great unwashed, perhaps even someone from a council estate in the city, putting his filthy trainers on the clubhouse carpet. Just as bad was the possibility of making the news. The members wouldn't like it. Exclusivity, privacy and discretion were the three granite pillars upon which his golf club stood. The addition of Joe and his very hairy dog in the lobby put the poor man into further paroxysms.

'I've already told your colleagues, there is nothing for you here. Nothing has been stolen. Whoever it was who triggered the alarm was seen driving off at high speed by my wife. Now please, will you go away before the press get wind of it. And take that monster with you.'

'Certainly, sir,' said Joe. 'I'll just take a look around outside, if I may.'

'I've told you, there is no need. And the Chief Constable is a member here.'

'I know that, sir. I also know that if I don't look around with my dog, my Chief Constable will have me scrambled on toast for breakfast and he'll be interested to find out why you stopped me looking. Now, if you'll excuse me. Sir.'

Around the back of the clubhouse, which had been built in the 1920s in the style of a Palladian mansion, was the professionals' shop. Regardless of the panicky steward's story, it had obviously been broken into. A window was smashed and there was golf gear and clothing all over the floor. Joe let Cass go free to have a sniff around and the dog wandered over to the first tee. For a moment he looked as if he was going to squat and Joe was almost disappointed to find that he had got some plastic bags with him, but that wasn't it. Cass had information in his nose and he was off, full tilt, down the fairway on the right-hand edge, close to the short rough.

The first hole on this course had a sharply angled bend to the left – a dog-leg, in fact – with a dense wood beyond, perfectly placed for the scratch player to over- or undershoot with his drive and for the high-handicap player to do the same with his second. The penalty for too long a hit was a lost ball in the wood and the undergrowth at its near edge was well trodden. Cass took no notice of the bend and ran into the trees, nose down, with Joe panting along some yards behind and losing ground. Deep within, where no golf ball ever reached, there was a stream flowing with a steep embankment either side. As Joe got there he tripped over a bag of clubs and a large umbrella and went head first down the bank. Scratched, muddy and wet, he shone his torch in time to see Cass glancing back at him briefly before carrying on. Clambering up the far slope, Joe put his head into some barbed wire, suffering more scratches with trickling blood, and at the top there was no sign of his dog. This was the peril of free tracking. You could lose your tracker.

Shining his torch again he saw two red and yellow spots, either the eyes of a wild creature of the forest or of a police dog impatiently waiting for him to catch up. Joe staggered on, the dog turned and ran further ahead, got to a lane and stopped. The track was gone. The thief must have had a car after all.

Twenty minutes later, a soiled, ragged and bloody police officer and an excited dog waited on the steps of the clubhouse for the steward to answer the doorbell.

'Here you are,' said Joe to a startled Captain Mainwaring in pyjamas. 'Brand-new set of clubs, top of the range; one bag; one golf umbrella. Slightly soiled, but they'll clean up. Property of the club professional. Shop's been broken into, by the way. I'll tell them at the station and they'll be round in the morning. Goodnight, sir. Brilliant dog, don't you think?'

* * * * *

The Children in Need display began with two large burglars dressed in long-sleeved striped jumpers and Dick Turpin masks, riding an ancient motorcycle combination. In the sidecar were two sacks with 'SWAG' written on them. They did two laps of the field, when a police dog van pulled in behind them with lights and horns, and Joe leaning out of the passenger window blowing an old police whistle. The baddies fired guns with extra-loud blanks as they were chased around several more laps, before charging their bike into some straw bales, jumping out and running in opposite directions.

Joe and Cass, Glen and Solo leaped out of the van. It was difficult to tell which of the burglars was investing the greater effort in his running. Cass's reputation went before him but so did Solo's, a dog that had had extra firearms training and so was an especially keen and determined biter.

The burglars were wearing protective sleeves under their stripy jumpers, but they were only thin and not very much use. The chase was short, the barking loud, the biting realistic. Still, it was for charity.

Next up was the handbag snatcher. Joe put a long and dirty mac over his uniform, donned sunglasses and a flat cap, and had an argument with a WPC in plain clothes in the crowd. She screamed blue murder as he ran into the middle of the field with her handbag, and Glen let Solo go. Joe pulled a sawn-off shotgun from beneath his mac, a real sawn-off that had once been used in a bank robbery, and fired a super-extra-loud blank. Kaboom! Solo never faltered in his stride. In firearms training, the next kaboom! is supposed to come with the dog about halfway to his man, but Joe made a mess of pulling the second trigger and Solo was almost on him when he fired. It went kaboom all right, but all it did to Solo was divert him from the arm with protective sleeve to the backside with protective dirty mac. Joe wanted to throw the gun down so Solo would let go, but dropping real firearms in public was a hanging offence.

Glen turned up grinning like the proverbial county cat. 'Get the ****ing thing off me,' whispered Joe, somewhat urgently. Glen laughed. 'I mean it, you bastard, get him off. Tell him the gun isn't loaded.' Glen still grinned while Solo's teeth sunk further into Joe.

'The only way I can get him off is to smack him in the ribs with my truncheon, which distracts him you see, but I can't do that in front of all these people, can I? Oh well, I'll see what I can do.' He grabbed Solo by the scruff and pulled, while Joe flung off the raincoat just as Solo relaunched his attack. He seemed content with the coat this time and happily ripped it into its component threads.

Vengeance is mine, saith the Lord, or in this case Joe's, because the next turn of the show featured Glen as a bicycle thief. A mini-skirted WPC rode the bike around the field once, then leaned it carefully against a straw bale before mincing off towards the beer tent. Glen, in tracksuit with hood over baseball cap, crept up and stole the machine, just as Joe and Cass appeared. Glen, fearing the worst, pedalled like mad but Cass had him in the right arm before he'd reached halfway across the grass and the three of them, Glen, Cass and bicycle, were soon in a flailing tangle. Joe ran frantically towards them. When he got there he beckoned, equally frantically, towards the beer tent. The same WPC and another emerged, wearing what might have passed for nurses' uniforms in a *Carry On* movie, or a strip club, carrying a stretcher. With much ado about everything, they got in a huddle and a muddle with the other participants, emerging eventually to run back to the beer tent with Cass on the stretcher.

Joe had seen his widower, he of the lost dress watch, in the crowd and went over for a word. 'Thank you so much,' said the man. 'I haven't laughed so much since... well, anyway, I thought it was great. I've had a pint of Old Newtstrangler, or something of the sort, and a hot pork sandwich with stuffing, and I've put some money in the tin, and do you know, I could have sworn that when your dog went past on the stretcher, he winked at me.'

* * * * *

The taxi driver on the rank at Clufford railway station described the incident as a quarrel. Two Asians had been arguing with a squat, heavily built white man in a leather jacket. The white man stormed off, got in his car and roared away in a huff. The two Asians had a heated discussion for a minute or two, then jumped in their car and also roared away, in pursuit.

The taxi driver hadn't got the numbers, or said he hadn't, but he did know what sort of cars they were. The Asian boys, described as 'well known around here' – code for drug dealers – had a souped-up Vauxhall Astra and the white man a BMW M3 Evolution, black, with smoked-glass windows.

If the taxi driver had said it was a pink-and-purple-striped Rolls-Royce Silver Shadow with lace curtains, registration FU 2, he could not have identified it more closely. Only one squat, heavily built white man known to the police in that area had a black M3, and that was Patrick Malone, sometimes referred to as Bugsy by people well out of earshot. This was a supermonster of a saloon car, nought to sixty in just over five seconds, capable of 170 mph with the limiter removed. While there were several M3s in ownership around the more leafy suburbs and much-sought-after villages, those owners were more likely to be at home with a glass of vintage port at half-past ten at night, rather than arguing on a street corner by Clufford station with two dodgy Asians. In any case, the leafy suburbians didn't have black ones, because that was a colour seemingly reserved for drug barons, also for those security-minded persons who provide extra protection for commercial premises whether their clients need it or no, and for those few pimps who rise in good health to the top of their profession. It was thought in police circles that Paddy Malone qualified for an M3 on all three counts.

The call went out. BMW M3, registration such and such, probably heading south. Do not approach driver without back-up. It's Paddy Malone.

The car was probably heading south because that was where he lived, between Clufford and the big city, and his obvious route was along the main road. A traffic cop spotted him going at one hell of a speed over the river bridge and swung in behind, which he'd have had to do for anyone going that fast. The Asian boys, observing from a distance, decided to call it a night and turned off. The traffic cop radioed the control room. He was following at speeds in excess of 100 mph and he hoped that another car was better placed ahead to cut the bastard off.

Glen Conway listened to the radio traffic in his van, parked in a field entrance about 15 miles south of Clufford. It didn't have much to do with him, yet, but he knew Paddy Malone all right. They all did. The next radio message was impossible to understand at first. The traffic cop, following Malone, had come across a scene of utter horror and been forced to abandon the pursuit. There was the body of an old woman, or most of a body, and pieces of dog. The body had two dog leads in one hand. They'd been hit by a car, obviously, in the centre of a village that had been bypassed but whose main street was still used as a short cut and rat run by locals.

The reconstruction later showed that the old lady had been crossing the village high street with her two dachshunds, as she always did at that time, to take them for a short walk to the green and back. As she emerged from behind a parked car, she and the dogs had died instantly, hit by the high-velocity vehicle later shown to have been the BMW M3 in question. It had to be later, because Malone didn't stop. He probably didn't even brake; there were no flat spots on his tyres. Very expensive, those tyres were.

Listening to the radio, Glen began to see a role in it for him. If the car had swiped the old lady and, by the sound of it, her dogs too, it would be a mess. The driver would be bailing out and making a run. If he was allowed to get home, he'd be able to deny all knowledge and say his car had been stolen. Glen took his van around the bypass and kept looking. The radio was alive with calls of every sort, except one saying the car had been seen.

That call came in just as Glen found it, parked half on the pavement in the next village with a big dent in the bonnet, the nearside headlight smashed and the keys still in. Black BMW M3 abandoned, said the radio, according to a phone call from a resident, Heckington Road, Musterby. One white male – leather jacket – and one white female – blonde, high-heeled shoes – observed by resident running from the scene.

Glen called in to say he was at the scene himself and had taken the keys out and locked them in his van. He was going to look for the two runaways but had little expectation of success. He put Solo in harness and set off in the direction the car had been going. People were still about on the street. The pubs were still open, the corner shop was just locking up. This was the hardest of hard-surface tracking. Solo had no way of telling which of the thousand smells was the one he should follow. Almost certainly, Malone and his girlfriend had flagged down a taxi or got someone to come and pick them up. They weren't the type to try escaping across the countryside. It was a lost cause after ten minutes and Glen called in to say so and, since it was well after his bedtime, he was going home.

Joe's phone rang at 5am. He was to attend a briefing at HQ on the Malone incident. Joe knew Malone better than most. In his earlier days with his first dog, he'd answered a call for back-up from a bobby who'd stopped a tearaway. This man, of stocky build and Caucasian extraction, appeared to have exempted himself from the regulations regarding motor insurance and road tax for his Porsche. Rather than say he'd forgotten, or he'd sent his girlfriend to do it, or it was in the post, this particular yobbo had threatened to kill all police officers as soon as he got the handcuffs off.

Like so many brave hearts, Malone soon calmed down at the sight of a German Shepherd's teeth and they took him in and booked him, whereupon he repeated his promise to reduce the establishment of the police force by as many as possible, using whichever weapons would cause the most pain. Nobody in that police station had any reason to doubt that Malone was quite capable of doing what he said, and now, after several years of what a business analyst might describe as aggressive marketing strategies, he was the region's drug tsar, in the sense of undisputed ruler and beneficiary of empire, doing 100 mph in an M3 and killing old ladies.

The intelligence they had on Malone suggested he could be at any one of four addresses, but the most likely was the girl's house. As the only dog handler there, Joe made sure that he and Cass would be going to that one, a small, modern block of flats on the east side of town. On a word from the radio, all four teams hit the spots at the same time.

As the door caved in, with Joe one step behind the very large sergeant leading the raid, an attractive if slightly brassy blonde appeared in a short nightie. She seemed rather dazed by the whole business and never asked what the police were doing knocking her door down. Joe sent Cass to search the flat but, apart from three personal vibrators and a couple of hundred quid in cash, it was clean as clean. In the stairwell space on the ground floor was a Honda Goldwing motorcycle which, a check on the national computer revealed, was registered to one Patrick Malone. Outside was a Peugeot hatchback, again with smoked-glass windows, registered to a female at this address, and inside it was some litter from a McDonald's take-away and a little black book full of names and telephone numbers and addresses.

Some of the names were very recognisable: pillars of the community, upright citizens whose selfless deeds often featured in the local paper. Some Joe knew as traders providing those goods and services to the public requiring complete discretion. Others he guessed would be ordinary consumers of same, or merchants, importers, runners and enforcers making up what looked like the entire sex, drugs and rock and roll industry across the region. A team of CID telesales people was going to have some fun with this.

Joe was convinced Malone was hiding somewhere close, despite the dog's behaviour indicating otherwise. It was a modern flat. There really were not many places a man could hide, but Joe had the feeling he was being watched, and it was Malone doing the watching. Such a feeling did not transmit to Cass, who wasn't bothered, so they had to give up.

Several weeks later, Malone surfaced in Bruges. The Belgian police lifted him and he was brought back to face what few charges had a chance of being proved but, defended by the very finest team of hook-wrigglers and loophole unveilers that British jurisprudence could furnish, nothing would stick.

Things move quickly in the world of opportunities inhabited by such as Paddy Malone. In those few short weeks his position as the one true king of pharmaceuticals had been challenged and eroded by eager competitors. There was confusion and uncertainty where before there had been clarity and simplicity. He set about rebuilding his business to its former commanding position and beyond, this time using a more delegated structure with several key executives in charge of defined geographical areas, each known by the name of the pub used as its control centre. Malone, company chairman and managing director, called them his franchises and claimed to have taken the idea from Colonel Sanders. Like the white-whiskered maestro of fried chicken, Paddy kept out of the daily details and concerned himself only with the broader issues. As in any large corporation, the broader issues were mainly to do with people.

He had a phone call one day from the landlord of the premises that were HQ for the Swan with Two Necks area. The franchisee was Educated Tony, a name he had acquired by claiming to have won a place to read philosophy at the University of Oxford, only to be prevented from taking it up by an unfortunate incarceration in a complicated case of grievous bodily harm. Educated Tony had been running a smoothly functioning and profitable operation and had been making substantial and steadily increasing returns on investment. However, one evening he had made some indiscreet remarks to a barmaid while under the influence of premium-strength lager. These remarks indicated a fine disregard for Mr Malone. Old Bugsy, apparently, was a man who had no idea about the amount of money being fiddled from under his nose. It was relatively easy to get to the top, was Educated Tony's opinion. The really hard part was staying there. Maybe His Imperial Highness Bugsy the First wasn't so secure on his throne as he thought.

The barmaid told the landlord and he, being Malone's spy (as were all the pub landlords in the circle) thought he'd better let the boss know what was going on. Malone jumped in his car, now a more respectable and middle-aged Jaguar but still distinguished by smoked glass.

From the window of his apartment, the indiscreet franchisee saw his boss draw up and went out to meet him, assuming it was an unscheduled but routine business meeting. Malone pulled a gun and shot Educated Tony three times, adding a fourth to the temple, a *coup de grâce*, as he lay dying on the pavement.

This was in broad daylight, in a residential district. People were looking out of their windows. Malone calmly got back in his car and drove home, slowing down briefly on a river bridge to throw the gun out of his car window, over the parapet, not giving a second thought to the old man there in the cap and raincoat, staring at the water. Thing was, this cap was sitting on the head of an ex-Para, Korean War, and he knew what the small black object was that had been chucked so carelessly from the driver's side of a Jaguar, and he went home and telephoned the police.

While waiting for the underwater search unit to arrive, and with only an hour or two before the scent on the gun wore off, Joe Sleightholm and Cass went to search the river banks, which were steep, overgrown and not intended for fishermen, policemen or any warm-blooded creatures other than the local small mammals. It was, indeed, a very good place to have thrown away a gun. Getting over – in Cass's case, through – the fence was the easy part. Setting the dog up to search would be more difficult, as Cass had little experience of impenetrable jungles, and the worst bit was going to be Joe trying to keep up with the dog to see if he indicated.

Joe struggled through brambles, nettles, cow parsley, docks, Japanese knotweed and goodness knows what else to get his back to the foundations of the bridge. 'Find,' he said to Cass, and the dog, brilliantly, did a very quick search of the pathway they had just made up to the top of the bank. 'Find, Cass,' said Joe, pointing into the jungle. The dog looked at Joe as if to say, 'What? In there?' and made a half-hearted, burrowing movement. It looked a bit too much like hard work.

Joe tried to gee him up with excitement in his voice. This was a difficult game but really, really important. 'Find, Cass, find, come on boy, find!' At last, in he went. Joe followed, calling encouragement to the dog, but could not keep in touch. He could hear rustling and he could see movement, but he could see no dog. The rustling stopped. Silence. Joe tried to follow where it looked as if Cass might have gone, but it was guesswork. Tarzan, the Last of the Mohicans or another dog could have followed, but not a simple policeman. He was blundering about, getting nowhere, when he heard more rustling and a bedraggled Cass appeared, covered in goosegrass and bits of bramble tangled in his mane and with a slightly impatient cast to his face. He could not have conveyed his message more clearly. Where have you been? Come on, you twerp. It's over here.

Normally on such a job, Joe would have wanted to be right up there with Cass to stop him picking up the gun and contaminating DNA and fingerprints. Cass was trained to indicate a find, not to pick it up, but alone in the jungle he might have reverted to retrieving mode.

After more crashing about in the wilderness, this time with Joe close by, Cass went down, or as near as he could on a bed of briars, and there it was: a 9 mm automatic. It would later be shown to have Malone's DNA and prints all over it, and to be the murder weapon.

Simple police work put the car at the murder scene and the ex-Para had seen the gun being thrown, but there was nothing forthcoming from the late Educated Tony's neighbours, after some of Malone's junior managers visited them. So confident was Malone that no witnesses would come forward to testify against him, he admitted he might have handled the gun when someone tried to sell it to him in a pub. The seller must have been trying to get his – Malone's – prints on the weapon so he could be framed for the murder. No, sorry, he couldn't remember which pub, nor anything about the would-be gun salesman. The police didn't feel they had quite enough yet to charge him, so he walked.

Malone decided to hold a wake for his dead friend at The Swan with Two Necks. The word went around and almost everyone who lived on the shady side of the street was there. Apologies were received from those who were unable to attend due to the guardians of Her Majesty's most secure lodging houses not considering a wake for a drug dealer sufficient reason for compassionate leave. Of course, the police were aware and they expected trouble. This was Malone's way of demonstrating his power. All the honoured guests knew who'd shot Educated Tony, and their attendance at the party was the equivalent of the dukes and earls swearing allegiance to the king in case they were next in line for the scaffold.

While acknowledging who was indeed the king, the aristocracy still had their own jealousies and squabbles, which suited Malone. A bit of 'divide and rule' never went amiss and he wasn't disappointed. The first few sabre-rattles went by without bloodshed but a police informant could see it wouldn't be long and made a coded phone call. By the time Joe and Cass turned up, the first fight had started, outside. Police already there delayed their action a little, hoping that one combatant would disable the other rather than having them both turn on the common enemy. Glasses and bottles started flying about inside the pub, windows were broken, men staggered through the doorway with wounds, and the police had no choice but to go in.

Cass had never seen anything like this before. Somehow, in all his time, he hadn't been on a public order job, not even to a football match. Joe was deeply concerned. There were more than enough villains in that pub to guarantee that knives would be carried by some. He'd been in plenty of disturbances in his pre-dog days. He knew that the uniform would make him a target in this company. His dog, so promising, so much a part of him and his life, could be stabbed. He could take a beating and a kicking, which would ruin him. Cass seemed to be eager to do something but, held on a short lead, only wagged his tail.

Joe was cautious. Cass was not prepared. Maybe they should

get involved. Maybe Joe should pay out some of the long leash and let Cass have more freedom, but if the mayhem makers didn't take any notice he might bite anyone, goodie or baddie. Some of the bobbies in the fight were taking hard knocks already. They wouldn't want Cass's teeth drawing their blood as well.

Cass's special nose for the great unwashed wasn't infallible and might well have been confused by the expensive perfumes some of the villains would be wearing. A man running, for instance, would always be a criminal to Cass, even if he were the Chief Constable, and so probably would be a man fighting. The result was, Joe and the dog did nothing.

Malone's case did come to court. His confidence had been misplaced. Witnesses were persuaded to testify. He had been seen shooting the man, he'd been seen driving the Jaguar; as well as the ex-Para on the bridge, a lady doctor had been behind him when he threw an object from the car that could have been a gun, and PC Sleightholm confirmed that the gun was found by his dog Cassius on the correct bank side to match the doctor's and the old man's evidence. The jury had no doubts and the judge made sure that Malone would qualify for his retirement pension before he saw freedom again.

This was all to the good, but Joe's indecision at The Swan with Two Necks had cost him some very sharp words indeed from the sergeant who had led the operation, an ex-dog handler who knew what was what. Joe's excuses — that the dog hadn't happened across that sort of thing before and couldn't tell friend from foe — met only with the obvious statement that he bloody well should be able to, so get something done about it.

Joe enlisted the aid of the full team of instructors at the dog school, each of them an expert in winding a dog up to full pitch. After a few exercises under the general heading of crowd control, with the instructors in plain clothes, Cass could be relied on to snarl, bark, snap, get up on his hind legs held back only by the leash, and generally put the fear of God into anybody misbehaving in a group.

The final exercise on this little extra course was for Joe and Cass to break through a barricade to confront and disperse the demonstrators beyond, or police-dog instructors shouting all kinds of rubbish and waving big sticks. Cass thought this was great and couldn't wait to get at them, so when Joe stuck his left boot into the barricade to try and shift it, Cass stuck his teeth into Joe's calf. He'd never done that before. Joe had had no idea how much a bite like that could hurt.

CHAPTER TWELVE

IF WE DO MEET AGAIN, WHY, WE SHALL SMILE

One time in his early days as a dog handler, before he met Cass, Joe had been sitting in his van doing nothing in particular when two lads went past on motorbikes. They were in a 30 limit, doing at least 60 and obviously racing. Joe pulled out, foot to the floor and, with maximum effort, got near enough to clock them at 70. He knew he'd lose them soon so he switched on the horns and lights and they pulled over.

Joe knew one of them. This was Jason Wellington, a noted thief who liked to be called Duke but was more usually known as Boots. His speciality in thievery was motorcycles and so Joe was quite surprised when the bike he was on had all its proper paperwork and a tax disc. He got another surprise when they pleaded not guilty to the speeding charges, which for Joe meant giving evidence, including the fact that he'd had the speedometer on his van checked immediately after the incident. The result was heavy fines and points for the speed merchants and a close watch being kept on Mr

Wellington. Despite receiving more police attention than the average member of the public, Boots Wellington prospered in his trade of unfair motorbike exchange to such an extent that he came to need a legitimate front, a visible means of support to explain his financial success. He opened a motorcycle retail unit on a new industrial estate that was being built on the wartime aerodrome where the hard-surface tracking training used to be held.

Wellington dealt only in top-of-the-range bikes, new or historically important. He also stocked the very finest leathers, the most expensive helmets, and all necessaries and accessories for the wealthy and/or obsessed motorcyclist. That he had funded his start-up from the proceeds of crime was never doubted, and whenever a superbike or other machine with special cachet went missing, his repair shop was the first place the police looked. He never had what they were seeking, and when they did occasionally happen across a dodgy bike he always had a plausible reason for it being there.

Wellington's business thrived. Although a fellow of his stamp never could resist the odd bit of dishonesty, he was doing so very well that he really had no need of it. By dint of his own knowledge and skills he astounded everybody, including himself, by making a great success of accidentally going straight.

The industrial estate was also growing and permanent security staff had to be employed. At about half-past eight one evening towards the end of September, a guard noticed something odd on his CCTV screens. There was a Transit van that hadn't been there last time he looked, so he pressed the police alarm and went to keep an eye on things from a safe distance.

If the cops had arrived quietly, with no headlights, they might have caught the burglars at it. Instead, an over-enthusiastic and inexperienced car crew turned the horns and the blue light on. Still, they had been very quick on the scene and soon picked up two suspicious characters who were running down a lane about a mile and a half away.

Joe Sleightholm and Cass had been half an hour distant when the call came. When they got there, an Audi had been noticed in a nearby hotel car park with one man sitting in it, chain smoking. Both the abandoned Transit and the Audi were registered in the same, somewhat seedy district of the major city in the neighbouring force's area, but the Audi man had come up with a reasonable story. His girlfriend was an exotic dancer – well, a strippergram, actually – and she'd been booked to strut her stuff at a private function in the hotel. He was taxi driver for the night.

The police thought it more likely that the Audi was a back-up car in case something went wrong with the motorcycle break-in. By the time they had checked the private functions at the hotel – there were two, one a freemasons' ladies' night and one a family party to celebrate grandma's eightieth – the Audi had roared off. More police stopped it some miles down the road. While the driver could not explain why, instead of an exotic girlfriend, he had a man in oily overalls hidden in the boot of his car, there was still very little to connect any of the four arrested men to the crime. There was a crime, attempted burglary, with doors forced, but no prize bikes missing. The security guard said he didn't think there were any good pictures of people on the CCTV.

The police might be able to show that the four men knew each other, that they all had previous, that the Transit van belonged to one of the men arrested running in the lane, that the man in overalls was a mechanic in a motorcycle racing team, but even if they could show that the gang was famous for thefts of the finest products of MV Augusta, Harley-Davidson and Ducati from garage showrooms on September evenings at half-past eight, none of it would stick in a court. It was all circumstantial.

Ladies and gentlemen of the jury, my clients have told you that their van was hijacked and they were made to run for their lives. You have heard the evidence that the mechanic was in the boot of the Audi to listen to a knocking sound that had worried the driver. The story of the exotic dancer is yet another example of an innocent man, suffering from police persecution and under stress, saying the first thing that comes into his head. Whoever tried to batter down that showroom door, it was not my clients and the police should be out looking for the true perpetrators.

Joe kitted Cass up in his harness and started by the showroom door, which had been heavily thumped with the 14 lb hammer left lying where it had been dropped. Cass was now a thoroughly experienced dog at the height of his powers, and proved it by picking up a track right away. Following it steadily, checking every now and again, he led Joe across the customer car park and the wide expanse of concrete where the delivery vehicles came and went. Onto a patch of grass he speeded up, then slowed again as he reached the old perimeter road, around which the bombers had taxied before setting off for Germany.

The airfield was bordered with farmland on three sides. Modern traffic on this stretch of tarmac was tractors, trailers and combines and there was a lot of mud about. In his torchlight, Joe could see footprints here and there, some of them very clearly marked.

As the perimeter road turned, Cass kept going on the same line, through a gate, into a field of stubble. The ground became harder and the footprints faded out, but Cass was quite sure where he was going. He led Joe to the far side of the field and along its edge until they reached a gate that opened on to the lane where Joe knew the first two men had been arrested.

He got on his radio and described where he was, with a row of four bungalows in front of him and an older house with a Victorian Royal Mail collection box let into the wall. This, he had confirmed to him by the arresting officer, was exactly the spot where the suspect pair had been taken up. Around a couple of corners and down the road a few hundred yards was the hotel where the Audi had been waiting in vain.

'That, Cass my old friend, was the confirmation track of tracks,' said Joe, the pride in his dog bringing tears to his eyes. 'New concrete, grass, ancient RAF tarmac, miles of it, and stubble. What a dog you are.' Unfortunately, as Joe very well knew, the evidence of a dog's nose is not considered proof. How could the ladies and gentlemen of the jury be sure that this very excellent dog was following the two men in the dock, my clients, and not a fox or a badger, or, indeed, any other person or persons unknown?

They walked back to their van. Cass jumped in and went to

sleep while Joe got out his roll of plastic bags, which had many purposes, including picking up after Cass when he committed an indiscretion on somebody's lawn. This was going to be a long job but, he was sure, worth it. Carefully retracing their route, Joe stopped at all the best footprints and placed a bag over each, securing the evidence with sticks and stones. He drew a plan of the route showing where the prints were, so that Scenes of Crime could go over it in the morning. Even a barrister of hallmarked silver tongue polished with honey would have difficulty explaining that little lot.

It was a senior administrative type at Broadcasting House who said, 'There's more to the BBC than broadcasting, you know', and Joe was about to find out that there was more to the police than policing. He went back on duty the next evening to hear the news that the four men had been released without charge and with no more chastisement for their sins than an uncomfortable night in the cells, which would hardly have been a new experience, nor a great inconvenience. And nobody had bothered to look at his footprints.

Joe was very, very annoyed. He talked to the other officers involved in the arrests. The opinion was unanimous. Here had been a gang of four professionals, travelling career criminals who could pop up anywhere and do any kind of burgling job, or worse possibly, and we'd had them locked up and ready for roasting and we'd let them go. They'd be laughing all the way to the bank, or whichever type of premises they were going to turn over next.

Somewhere in the police service – behind locked doors on a

planet far, far away from the one Joe worked on – were officers whose appointments did not consist of handcuffs, truncheon and radio but of calculator, spreadsheet and budgetary targets. These people had decided that this was not an opportunity to put away a dedicated group of practised criminals after all. It was, instead, only an attempted break-in, on a non-dwelling, featuring two vehicles from another force's area and four men ditto. According to the numbers and the pound signs, statistically it was not worth going for.

The effect on the morale and motivation of front-line police did not enter into the calculation, although Joe could take some satisfaction from the expense Boots Wellington would incur making his showroom more secure, with the generous quantity of police advice that was part of the service after a break-in. I'll have to nip round there one day, thought Joe, and tell Boots about the footprints.

* * * * *

The season of mists and mellow fruitfulness was also the season of political party conferences. Ever since the Provisional IRA bombed the Grand Hotel at Brighton in 1984, security at these conferences had become a massive operation with every kind of law enforcement agency involved, right the way down to every available dog handler including, when the circus came north, PC Joe Sleightholm and his dog. The scheme was twelve-hour shifts, two hours on and one off, covering a designated area of the sea front and wherever else was considered important.

Nothing ever happened. Someone might spot a seal swimming in the bay, but that was about it for excitement. The food was good, the overtime rates made it financially rewarding, but hell it was boring. Cass didn't like it, sitting there doing nothing, and Joe was on edge all the time in case some innocent came up wanting to stroke the nice doggy woggy diddums. If the sun shone, as it sometimes did in October, Joe could persuade himself that there were worse things to do than being paid to stroll along the prom, prom, prom. When the rain fell, the wind blew and the waves crashed against the sea wall, and the police were the only folk daft enough to be out (because they had to be), well, then you could wish for your dog van and your flask of coffee on your ordinary PC's wages.

This was Joe and Cass's second conference. The first one had been the party in opposition. This was the party in government, and they met the Home Secretary. In the better weather it was quite usual for the politicians to go walkabout, talking to the police. For some of them it was a bit of obligatory slumming, pressing the flesh and so on, while some saw it as a research opportunity. Perhaps they might pick something up from these ordinary coppers-in-the-street that they could use to embarrass their opponents. Some, like Michael Heseltine for instance, and Tony Benn, Joe found very genuine, interested in what he had to say and quite happy to chat about anything at all, whether it was in the papers, on the television or walking past in a short skirt.

Joe and Cass were standing by the promenade railings. There were a few police about, including a WPC who perhaps might have been better employed as an actress or model, and who had been asking Joe every morning if she could stroke Cass. Joe had told her no, because he might bite, but she wouldn't have it, saying that of course a police dog wouldn't bite a police officer. She'd just been going over the same argument when Joe spotted, in the distance but walking towards them in a determined way with a huge beam on his face, the current Home Secretary.

'Oh shit,' said Joe, 'look who's here.' He set about looping Cass's lead through the railings, middle one then top one, looking for a pulley effect. He tested it gently. Yes, he could hold Cass easily and, with a stronger yank, he'd be able to pull him back without the dog being able to get up on his hind legs.

The WPC trotted off to stand in line with the other half-dozen police, ready to be inspected by the incumbent Lord High Executioner, as if it were HM Queen meeting the England cricket team. The sergeant went along, introducing, and the Home Sec shook hands and asked a few banal questions, the beam never waning for a moment. A man known for his appetites and preferences, he spent a touch too long talking to the rather glamorous and flirty WPC who, from the look on the sergeant's face, was going to be given a lecture later on professionalism.

At the end of the line, the sergeant stood as if that was that, more or less blocking the way to Joe. The Home Secretary said, 'What about him?' and set off again, hand outstretched, beam fixed. The sergeant began a protest, something like, 'Er, um, well, I shouldn't...' but it was too late.

From Cass's point of view, here came a threat. Perhaps it was his special sensitivity regarding rats and other large rodents that cranked him up. Perhaps he couldn't stand smarmy gits. Perhaps his hackles rose as he sensed the insincerity dripping from one of the more odious holders of the post of Home Secretary in recent times.

Probably he felt Joe's discomfort and trepidation at the possibility of Death by Big Bossman. There was no precedent that Joe knew of, but he would have liked to bet that police dog handlers whose dogs drew the blood of Cabinet ministers were seldom awarded the OBE for it. In any event, Cass wasn't having this grinning turnip heading for his friend and master, with right hand to the fore like he'd seen in firearms training. He let off a sharp volley of his best and deepest barks and launched himself at Her Majesty's Secretary of State for the Home Department with his teeth glinting in the sunlight. That the result of the launch was a kind of backwards leap, as Joe hauled on the lead, did nothing to improve the Home Sec's opinion of it. His beam was replaced by a look, first of terrified, wide-eyed, Baskervillian panic, developing into the expression that meant, 'Ah, yes, of course, I realise he's only joking, ha ha, I hope I haven't wet myself', and on into a rapid recovery of the professionally smooth poise, a smart turn on the heel and a 'Good day to you all, keep up the excellent work, finest police force in the world and, obviously, the very finest of police dogs.'

'Terribly sorry, sir,' said the sergeant. 'I'm sure, he's never done that before.'

The insistent WPC came over but kept her distance. 'I have a cunning plan,' she said. 'See you tomorrow morning. He won't have a go at me. You'll see.'

The cunning plan was revealed the next day as six cooked sausages filched from the breakfast canteen. Cass liked the smell of them and the look of them. He sat quietly to eat them one by one, and jolly good they were. When the last was gone, the WPC stretched out her hand to pat him, and he bit her on the middle finger – not hard, but enough to make the pretty lady swear.

'I didn't know you knew words like that,' said Joe.

'I don't,' said the WPC. 'I've never done that before. Do you want to go for a drink after? Don't bring that ****ing dog.'

* * * * *

Christmas in Clufford for dog handlers meant foot patrols around the town's main shopping streets. Even in our era of credit cards there was still a lot of cash about, and the traditional accompaniment to cash is robbery. Cassius, being an egalitarian kind of a dog, held an equally low opinion of any stranger who tried to invade his personal space or, even worse, who seemed to his security-conscious mind a cause for concern. It had been proved that such a stranger could be the Home Secretary. Similarly, it could be any other cabinet minister, shadow minister or backbencher for that matter, or it might be Mrs Oswaldtwistle, high on shopping, or Mr Oswaldtwistle, his judgement impaired by serial pints of bitter while she went to the shops, or vice versa.

Some dog handlers made Christmas into a public relations exercise. If one had a dog that actually liked being petted, or would put up with it, he might spend some of his patrol time standing on a corner, chatting to passers-by, but not Joe and Cass.

They were constantly on the move, looking as busy as possible, in the hope of avoiding any Home Secretary-style incidents. Around six hours of proceeding at the regulation pace of two and a half miles an hour was fifteen miles, and Joe probably went a bit faster with Cass, so say eighteen miles up and down the cold and wet December streets of Clufford might make a saint feel a little scratchy by the end of it.

When a man, quite an old man, in a flat cap and mackintosh came up to Joe to ask the time, Cass growled at him and showed his teeth. Joe kept walking, told the man it was nearly five o'clock and apologised for Cass, saying it had been a long day and making a weak joke about being dog tired. With only another few minutes to do, Joe headed back to the police station. He put Cass in the van and popped in the station to see if there was any gossip. The WPC on the desk called him over.

'Joe,' she said, 'there's been a complaint, and I don't quite know what to do with it. Maybe I should ask the inspector.'

'What sort of complaint? About me?' said Joe.

'Not exactly. You see, this man came in, and he stood in front of me here, and took his cap off, and said he wished to lodge a grievance.'

'Lodge a grievance? What's that when it's at home?'

'He said he had a grievance concerning the abrupt nature of a police dog, and wished to lodge it. "A police dog?" I said. "What did it look like?" He said it was a very hairy one, so I knew it was yours.'

'Oh no. I bet I know who that was. Not very tall, about seventy, brown mac?'

'That's him. So I asked him to clarify the matter. Was he complaining about the police officer with the dog, or the dog itself? He said the police officer had been fine, nothing wrong with the police officer, but the dog had been abrupt. "Well," I said, "we have all sorts of forms and paperwork here, for recording evidence and everything, in duplicate and quadruplicate, including complaints from the public, but I don't have a form for lodging a grievance about an abrupt dog." He didn't look happy. I think he thought I was taking the piss.'

After the traditional Christmas shopping patrols came the traditional Boxing Day football match, Clufford Town against local rivals Blackstock, two teams that had hardly ever been out of the second tier of English league football since the grass grew. Promotion never featured for either of them and relegation, although often a worry, rarely happened either. The annual fixture list of the Football League was thus long established as tidings of comfort and joy for the police of the fortunate town whose side was due to be travelling away that year.

For those at home, it was their turn to handle the bother there was bound to be. Occasionally the whole thing passed off without incident but usually there would be a disputed penalty or a sending-off or some such, which would enrage one set of fans or the other. A few lads would start up and you could suddenly have a riot to contain.

This year the match was at the Pasture Lane ground, home of Clufford Town. It was a nil-nil draw and the football so awful that no supporter of either side could possibly have got worked up about it. The local radio commentator said that all the spectators must have committed a mortal sin over the holiday and this was God's punishment for it. The Blackstock fans mostly climbed back in their cars and coaches and went home to something more cheerful, while a large group of them, as they always did, walked from the stadium to the town centre, where the pubs were expecting them. Nothing would happen unless the Clufford lads decided to confront them but, as quite a few had left the match early to get into the pubs first, the signs were not good.

The main square in Clufford had six pubs. One, which was also a rather smart hotel, would not let anyone in wearing a football shirt, or a scarf or any other indication of allegiance to either side. Another, which had become a gastropub and didn't sell lager, was therefore of no interest, leaving four to extract as much money as possible from the madding crowd before things turned ugly, which Joe thought was the way it was going.

Drinkers and drunks were spilling on to the street, Blackstock lads on the far side of the square, Clufford lads on this. By the look of it, there would soon be jeering, chanting and taunting, followed by throwing of objects, followed by charging. Police reinforcements were arriving and were led, Joe was disappointed to see, by a sergeant known for his enjoyment of riots. Instead of exercising restraint and diplomacy in the hope of averting bloodshed, he would rather let things develop into a punch-up so he could whack a few participants and get some arrests out of it.

Cass was getting excited too, and Joe was getting worried. Although police manpower was increasing, he couldn't see any more dog handlers anywhere. If the fight kicked off soon, he'd be the only one. But no. Here came a dog van, blue light flashing, horns going, squealing to a stop in the centre of the square. Everybody stopped to look. Silence fell as the horns and light were switched off.

It was Glen Conway. Profession: dog handler. Ambition: to be a farmer. He'd already gone some way towards that target with a smallholding out in the hills somewhere. He jumped from the van, ran around the back, opened up, but instead of Solo a large and fat black-faced ewe jumped out, held by Glen on a police-issue lead and check chain.

Everybody fell about laughing except the sergeant. Glen tied his sheep to a lamp-post and there wasn't a single spark of trouble for the rest of the night.

* * * * *

The new year passed and word went about the dog handlers that it had finally been decided, by those whose offices had carpets, that it was their force's turn to represent police dogs at Crufts. What to do and who would do it was a matter delegated to Sergeant McKay.

The expected and probably most sensible thing would have been for Mac to do the display himself with Brutus. He was the most experienced man at trials and shows and that sort of thing. Although Brutus wasn't the best street dog, he was very good at training exercises. None of the other dog handlers could have complained about favouritism or injustice, because Mac the boss would have had all the grumbling and mickey-taking aimed at him. Instead, what he did was approach Joe Sleightholm.

'I want you to perfect a routine, Joe,' he said, 'for a show.'

'All right, Mac, but what show's it for?'

'We're doing Crufts this year.'

'So I heard,' said Joe. 'What's that to do with me? Oh no. No, you don't. You're not sliding out of it like that. Crufts main arena? Television? You do it.'

'It's an honour, Joe. For Cass. Mainly. Mainly for Cass. With a bit for you.'

The Crufts show was second week in March or thereabouts. They had half of January and all of February to train. They'd be off normal duties and Joe could have any help he wanted. Before that, they had a week of nights to finish.

It was almost a nightly experience in the control room to be passed a call from an anonymous well-wisher saying that someone was leaving a pub to drive home over the limit. Often the calls were hoaxes, or a form of practical joke on a person who'd been drinking orange juice, or they were revenge for a wrong done by the driver on the caller. Or, they were a way for some unfortunate twisted soul to get his kicks. Or, sometimes, they were genuine calls about a genuine danger to the public.

In any case, the police were obliged to investigate and this call was unusually detailed, giving the make, model and colour of the vehicle, the registration, the appearance of the driver and his passenger, and the brands and amounts of strong lager and Irish whiskey that said driver had consumed. The caller was a woman, the pub was way out in the sticks, and there was no need for the driver's name. The police knew exactly who he was.

Everyone called him The Colonel, because he affected the neat moustache, military bearing and what he imagined to be the apparel of choice of the retired army officer – being Kangol cap, Harris tweed jacket with leather elbow patches, lemon cashmere V-neck, Vyella shirt with heather-mixture tie, cavalry-twill trousers, hand-made brown brogues polished to a reflective sheen and ivory-handled walking stick. He lived in the old rectory of a village a few miles from the pub in question and saw himself as the squire. If asked what he did, he would say he was 'in property' – which was true to an extent, in that he owned some flats in Clufford that he rented – but his main income didn't come from that. It couldn't. He was clearly and obviously very wealthy. There had to be more than a few rented flats but what it was had baffled the police for as long as anyone could remember. There were all kinds of rumours: IRA, prostitution, illegal immigrants, but never drugs. The CID believed him to be a background villain, a financial Mr Big who planned and funded criminal enterprises well off his own patch, but of evidence there was no shred.

His habit was to go for a few drinks early on, before the dinner prepared by his live-in Mrs Bridges, in one of several country pubs within easy distance from home. He either had his son with him, allegedly as driver, or one of the many fluffy, well-put-together young ladies who found something attractive about him. There were times when he forgot about dinner and kept drinking, which he'd done on this evening, with his son. He was no different to many men in that the more he had to drink, the wittier he thought he was and, as he moved from the Stella to the Irish at eight o'clock, he started to pick on the barmaid – a pretty, young, dark-haired girl, Spanish-looking – who'd just come on.

He'd seen her before but not especially noticed, his attentions previously having been devoted to whichever fluffy young lady he'd had with him. Tonight there was no bit of fluff.

'Yes sir?' said the barmaid chirpily, perhaps not showing the requisite amount of deference.

'Do you have a large Black Bush?' said The Colonel, loudly so everyone could hear, following his jest with an even louder laugh. Coarse remark followed coarse remark and by the time he ordered one for the road, the barmaid had decided that here was the most obnoxious man she had ever met in her life.

'Are you sure you ought to drive, dad?' said the son, quietly.

'Don't be a boring little toad,' said the father, not so quietly. 'I've told you before about criticising me in public. The words side, bread and butter spring to mind, what?'

The barmaid popped outside for a moment with her mobile, dialled 999, read as much information as she could off the massive four-wheel-drive jeep that she knew was The Colonel's and undid two buttons on her blouse. A generous flash of cleavage, as she bent to retrieve a glass from under the counter, was enough to persuade The Colonel that he should have another large whiskey, and to allow time for a traffic car to park unobtrusively down the road to The Colonel's village.

The traffic cop's mistake became apparent as the 4WD swept past with The Colonel at the wheel and the son in the passenger seat. The police car pulled out and turned everything on, and the jeep kept going. Damn it. Should have done him at the pub, but it was too late now so the police settled into the chase.

Joe had been listening to the story on his radio, not seeing anything in it for him until now. A car chase with drunks in the lead often ended with the need for a dog, so he set off. The traffic cop, torn between the need to stop The Colonel before there was an accident and the need not to cause one by over-aggressive pursuit, followed his quarry home, where The Colonel stopped. The traffic cop got out and the jeep roared off again. OK, something had to be done, so when the jeep came to a roundabout the police car pulled alongside and tried to force The Colonel to stop. He wasn't having it, gave the police car a deliberate shunt sideways, did a very quick reverse, went the wrong way around the island and turned down a single-track lane. If anything had been coming the other way there would have been the most horrendous collision and, if the 'anything' had been a normal car rather than a bus or a tractor, it would have been crushed to a cube with whoever was inside it.

The lane took a sharp left but the jeep carried straight on into a ploughed field. The police car couldn't go there and the traffic cop had to watch as the jeep bumped and jumped across the furrows and into the distance. Joe was now a few minutes away and radioed the traffic cop, who was distraught after losing his man and thinking about what might have happened. He seemed to think that the 4WD would make it across the field and into the road beyond. Joe thought he was possibly overestimating the capabilities of vehicle and driver but went to have a look just the same, as did several other units. There wasn't much else happening that night and the lost driver was an A-list celebrity.

Joe tootled quietly along the lane that the jeep would

supposedly reach, saw nothing, and reversed up a farm track. Turning off engine and headlights, he listened with windows down for any sound of a jeep bouncing across a field. All he could hear on a very still night was the faint and distant natter of police radios. If only he'd known he was at that moment about a hundred yards from the wanted vehicle, a great deal of time and effort could have been saved. But he didn't know.

Hang on a minute, thought Joe. No matter what type of off-road vehicle it is, it's surely not going to get all the way across a big ploughed field that very likely has a ditch or two in it. The driver is drunk and excited. He's not going to see a ditch coming up, and if he does get stuck he'll never get going again. Best thing will be to go back to where he entered the field and track him from there. As Joe started up his van he heard Mac McKay's voice on the radio. Joe's boss was on his way. Well, if Joe needed an incentive, there it was.

At the point of entry to the field, Joe changed into wellies and set off with a torch and Cass on the lead. It was not exactly difficult to follow the 4WD's route. There were deep ruts made by tyres costing thousands of pounds a set. Before very long the ruts got deeper as the vehicle had hit a softer area of ground and there, sitting up to its axles in the dim moonlight, was the kind of 4WD they show on the adverts crossing the savannah, sweeping up and down Sahara dunes and splashing through fords on the Amazon. Alas, an English ploughed field in late January had proved too much for it.

Joe saw two sets of footprints continuing away in the same direction and, without bothering to look any further or seek the opinion of his dog, Joe followed them by torchlight until they were almost at the lane which it had been predicted the jeep would reach. No more than ten yards away from tarmac, the footprints stopped. This, Joe now realised, was very close to where he'd been parked in the farm track. They must have seen or heard Joe before, and turned back.

Cass hadn't had much to do until now. He'd been let off the lead and was wandering about, miffed that he hadn't been given a job of work, so Joe called him, apologised and gave him a 'Where is he?' That was better. Cass soon picked up the second set of prints that led back to the 4WD, where much trampling of the soil, previously missed by Joe in his haste, indicated that they'd tried to push the car out of its hole on their return, decided that it was useless, and made a run for it. But where?

Without any instruction from Joe, Cass ran around the vehicle, clockwise of course, found the track and the footprints and was off. Joe, in wellies, struggled to keep up and couldn't, until he came to a really thick old hedge that Cass was desperately trying to get through. The two men must have got through it, goodness knows how, and with Joe's help so did Cass; then he was away again, leaving Joe to sort out his own problems.

When he too managed it, he found himself in a field of six-foot weeds – or were they reeds? That was it. The farmer must have been growing new giant strains of Norfolk reed for thatched cottages. The ground was boggy enough anyway, and Cass was far, far ahead, and Joe began to feel a real concern for the men. It had been a long chase through difficult country. Cass would be highly delighted to find his quarry and could well show it.

Joe tried to shout, 'Stand still or I will send the dog', but failed. 'This is the police,' he tried again, with better results. 'Stand still or I will send the dog.' The call echoed around. He was in a lowish, flat, small valley. Beneath his feet it was wet and sinking. There must be a river somewhere. There must be a dog somewhere, come to that. Cass had disappeared and Joe didn't see him until he got to the end of the reeds, on to a minor road, and shone his torch into the next field.

What he saw was not so much a tracking dog as a hunting dog. Cass was in hot pursuit, in a wide semi-circle, hurtling along on what was clearly a very fresh trail. When he came back to the road he crossed it without hesitation and disappeared again, on the same side they'd just been on. Joe ran for the place Cass had crossed and found a pair of five-bar gates. One led into grassland, the other into an electricity transformer station, a small compound surrounded by a high metal fence and with signs saying 'Danger of death'. Cass was out of sight but not out of hearing, and Joe heard a bark seemingly coming from the far side of the compound. He'd found at least one of the men and Joe was wondering which five-bar gate to climb over when the son appeared inside the compound and came up to that gate, while Cass appeared in the field and leaped over his gate to put his front paws on the top rail of the other one and do a new version of find-and-speak, open-person.

GSDs, and most dogs, do not take naturally to leaping over five-bar gates. They will always try to go under or through and it takes a lot of training to persuade them over. Even then they won't usually do it operationally unless the handler is there to give lots of encouragement. Cass had done it twice on his own, without a second thought. Joe was very proud.

What must have happened was the son had climbed his gate into the compound, realised he couldn't get out and, with Cass barking at him from the other side of the metal fence, realised the game was up. He claimed he had been the only one in the 4WD. Joe called up the traffic car, which turned up and took the lad away back to the family residence. He hadn't broken any law: being the son of his father was not an offence. Also turning up was Sergeant McKay.

'Where's The Colonel?' he said. 'What kind of a dog is that you've got, Joe? Hey you,' he shouted to the sky. 'This is the police. Come out or I'll send a real dog to get you, and he bites like buggery.'

'Get lost, Sarge,' said Joe. 'This is our show.'

'Come on, Joe. Where do you think he's gone, The Colonel?'

The best guess was that he'd doubled back with his son and kept going, which put him somewhere between where they were standing and the marshland. If not, he could be anywhere, left, right or behind.

'All right,' said Mac. 'You go that way. Me and Brutus'll try the other options.'

Cass had a sniff up and down the lane and decided on a route going back in the general direction of the 4WD. Joe foresaw another chase through the reeds, through that thick hedge and across hundreds of yards of ploughed field. Whatever else The Colonel might be, he was bloody fit.

Cass was not back-tracking, however. He had a new line,

veering off to the left and, instead of the marsh, they came to the river. It was a slow-flowing cutting, more of a big drainage channel than a river, and Cass ran along the side of it. They'd gone 50 yards or so when Joe saw a clump of turf and soil floating in the water.

'Good lad,' said Joe, excitedly. 'Where is he?' Cass ran further along the bank and turned sharp right over the stream. When Joe caught up he found a farmer's bridge, a construction of ancient railway sleepers with grass growing on it, and Cass was crossing and recrossing this little bridge, tail up, everything about him saying he'd found, but unable to move his knowledge any further. At last he sensed something else, went down the river bank a way among the undergrowth, and let off a huge bark that echoed all the way around that valley. Mac, the traffic cop with the son, and everybody else heard, and knew The Colonel had been caught.

Joe lay Cassius down, knelt on the bridge and peered under it with his torch. There, wedged in a very small gap, and once more proving Sleightholm's Law, was The Colonel. He took no notice of Joe's instruction to get out.

'It is half-past twelve at night. You're stuck. Now get out, or I'll send my dog to drag you out.' No movement. 'I need a sample of your breath, which you are required to give me by law. If you refuse, it counts the same as if you're guilty. So come on.' Nothing. 'This is absolutely your last chance, and my dog will not care which bit of you he gets hold of.'

Reluctantly, The Colonel crawled from his cramped position, stood up on the grass beside the stream and keeled over backwards, holding his hand to his heart and making a few waffling noises. He lay there, prone and silent.

'Get up, you daft twat,' said Joe. 'I've seen better acting at my daughter's nativity play.' No answer. Nothing stirred. Joe thought back to his first-aid training and Dr ABC: danger, reaction, airway, breathing, circulation. They were in no danger so it had to be reaction. Joe looked at Cass, lying with his head on his front paws. The dog could get a reaction all right, but no, much as he'd like to, in the circumstances Joe had better try something less drastic. He pinched a half inch on the back of The Colonel's hand and got a squeak.

'Now, listen to me, O great one. As already stated, I require you to provide me with a sample of your breath. If you refuse you will be prosecuted and banned for at least a year, and everybody will think you're a complete arsehole. Good. Thank you.'

Joe, with Cass on the lead, strolled along the river bank with The Colonel in front, looking rather pathetic. The traffic cop was back there, anxious to witness the event, and so was Mac, who told The Colonel how lucky he was that he'd only had Cassius after him and not Brutus as well. The traffic cop breathalysed him – he was over – and took him away to be processed. There was jubilation all around. What a terrific night for the police dog handlers and especially for a certain long-haired hound, whose devotion to duty, including five-bar gates, had been exceptional even by his own standards.

They got back to the station about an hour later to find The Colonel still sitting there. A quiet night had suddenly turned into rush hour and the custody sergeant was overwhelmed. When he did get to The Colonel to put him on the machine, it was nearly two o'clock, three hours and more after his last drink. The roadside tester, the alcometer, was regarded as an indication only, sufficient to warrant arrest. The machine in the police station, much more accurate, gave the reading that would be used in evidence.

He blew, and he was marginally under. It was so close, the difference could have been in that 5% of alcohol that leaves the body in sweat. The Colonel had certainly been sweating, but he was sweating no more. His face changed from pure relief to pure spite.

'Just you wait, copper, you and your ****ing pooch,' he hissed at Joe. 'Wait 'til my lawyers get hold of you. They'll do more than bite your arse.'

Joe could hardly believe it. 'You win some, you lose some' didn't really cover this situation. All that carry-on, and no result. The bastard was away. Justice? No such thing, apparently.

There was better news in a day or two. The Colonel had had to pay a tow-truck man £500 to get his 4WD out of the field, and another £500 to the farmer for permission to get his car out of said field – or compensation for soil damage, as the farmer called it – and he was to be charged with reckless driving. Being The Colonel he was going to plead not guilty and elect for trial by jury at the Crown Court. A year later, with the accused defending himself as there was not a barrister in the land who knew as much about the job as he did, the case would be heard. Joe, Mac and the traffic cop would be there, and the barmaid, before a judge who would patently be irritated by the arrogance of the amateur lawyer, waving maps about, quoting braking distances and generally implying the natural tendency of all police officers to make up fairy stories and to persecute law-abiding individuals such as himself.

The Colonel would be found guilty, fined £1,000 and banned for eighteen months. Not much, all in all, but a lot better than nothing.

CHAPTER THIRTEEN

SICK OF MANY
GRIEFS

J oe and Cass were on nights, in the van, about as far away as
they could have been, when the call came through about a
burglar disturbed. Any tracks were an hour old and possibly too
far gone by the time they got to the rather select area of large
detached houses and, with Cass on the lead, walking up to the
one that had been done, they came to a Reliant Robin van.

Maybe the worries about Crufts had temporarily disabled
those parts of his brain connected with copper's intuition, but it
never occurred to Joe to ask himself why there might be a Reliant
Robin, and a pretty beat-up one at that, in such a street at such a
time of night, nor did he take any notice of the little twitch of
Cass's head as they passed it.

They searched the garden of the burgled house and both the
next-door gardens. Nothing. Not the slightest expression of
interest from the dog. Joe decided to go back to where they'd
been, but he hadn't driven above two miles when another call

came. A burglar, presumably the same one because not many of that trade have the skill and nerve to pursue it at night in occupied premises, had been disturbed in a house not far from the first place. This fellow must be a bit of a twit, thought Joe as he turned round. Or he's very heavy footed for one of his calling.

Various units and the helicopter reported that they were on their way, but Joe and Cass were there before any of them. The house owner showed Joe the lounge window where the man had got out, with a large expanse of lawn beyond. Cass was on it immediately, free tracking, and right through a thick hedge of Leylandii. Beyond that was a lowish, woven wood fence. He was over that, and Joe was panting behind, across the next garden, over another fence, and another. If I'd wanted to run in the Grand National, Joe thought, I'd have brought a horse with me. The next fence was higher, though just manageable, but the next was a ten-footer. Cass wanted to get over but couldn't. The burglar was obviously something of an athlete.

Joe called Cass and went around the front of the house, where he met a sergeant and numerous bobbies. The helicopter was there too. The dog was running about, trying to pin down some elusive, half-understood information. The police officers stood still. They didn't want to be mistaken for anything Cass might want to bite.

Joe told the sergeant about the chase and why it had come to a stop. The helicopter observer radioed to say that they were going to stop too, not being able to find anything, when Joe noticed Cass. He was standing beside the double garage with his nose up.

'Tell that helicopter not to go,' he said to the sergeant. 'We've found the bastard.'

'What?'

'Tell him. Tell him quick.' Joe was away, opening the gate to the passage between garage and house that led to the back garden. Cass was ahead of him, trying to run and stand on his hind legs at the same time.

The back lawn was like a miniature cemetery. All over it were roof slates, sticking upright from the ground like little headstones. The neighbours were out next door and next door to that. Most people do come out to see what's happening when there's a helicopter hovering above, although some ring 999 to complain about the noise.

Cass looked up and barked. Joe shone his torch and shouted into his radio, 'He's up, he's up!' And there he was, frantically pulling slates off the roof and hurling them anywhere, in a futile attempt to burrow into the roof space. More officers arrived, a ladder was found and the burglar went quietly, asking if somebody would be so kind as to drive his Reliant Robin van back to the station.

Joe went for a pint with the helicopter observer a few days later. They were terribly expensive things, helicopters, were they not? But useful, in clear weather, when it wasn't raining, and there were no trees, and the fugitive wasn't hiding in a car or a corrugated-iron shed, or a greenhouse, but Joe hadn't realised that if someone was standing on a roof, the imaging gear couldn't see him.

It wasn't that, apparently. It was because all those houses had chimneys and central heating flues; it was a cool night, they'd all had their fires and boilers on and the smoke and steam outlets had shown as hot spots.

'What, so you thought the baddie was a central-heating pipe? I tell you what, my dog can tell the difference between a chimney and a chimney sweep any day of the week. Your round, I think.'

* * * * *

The routine Joe had devised for Crufts kept to the elements that looked impressive but were not so hard to do. The mantra was KISS: Keep It Simple, Stupid. The first exercise consisted of marching up and down and turning, with a mixtures of sits, stands, downs and down-stays, finishing with a smart heel. Next was distance control, with hand signals only to the dog on the other side of the arena: right arm out to the side, dog stood; point down, dog went down; to side, stood; point up, sat; both arms out and he came to Joe; hands together and he sat neatly in front; and heel.

Retrieving the wooden dumb-bell was followed by the jumps one at a time and all together, none of it in itself very difficult but looking very good when done with military precision. Obedience, retrieve and agility would normally have been enough but Joe wanted to finish on a flourish and so he decided to ask Lanky Laing to help him on a condensed, more showy version of the chase-and-stand-off exercise. Cass would sit beside Joe, off the lead in the middle of the arena, and Lanky would leap from the audience, shouting through a megaphone, 'Down with

Crufts, down with dogs, up with cats and goldfish', or some such
rubbish. He would run around the edge of the arena, still
shouting and waving, and Cass would be itching to go but would
not until given the command.

Joe would shout, 'Stand still or I will send the dog', Lanky
would keep running, so Joe would shout again, and then give
him, 'This is absolutely your last chance. Don't say I didn't warn
you. Stand still or I'll send the dog' and set the dog away with a
'Hold him.' Lanky would stop running and get on his knees in a
praying position, and Cass would do the perfect stand-off.

The problem Joe foresaw was to do with the size of the arena.
It was likely that there wouldn't be enough room for Cass to be
running hard while Lanky stopped the usual 20 yards away. If the
crazy man with the megaphone was too near, Cass would pile
straight in and bite him, rather than veering off to the side with
ears and tail up and doing his bouncing bark. Even better would
be if Cass circled Lanky, barking to keep him contained until Joe
arrived. Joe went to see his ex-Met mate, PC Laing.

'Fancy a trip dahn Lannan, Lanky?' said Joe.

'Not with a northern oik like you, Joe. This is about Crufts,
isn't it? Well, I'm not training your dog for you. Your dog. You do
it. I've got enough to do, trying to teach these heathens up here
the Queen's English.'

'You know what time it is when there's a pork pie on Clufford
town hall clock tower?'

'Yes, summat to ate, now piss off.'

Joe could keep Cass still while Lanky ran past, and all went
well until Lanky, as criminal, stopped and waited seven or eight

yards away. Cass, with no hesitation at all, kept running, bit Lanky on the right arm, and hung on with his teeth – they were not actually piercing the leather sleeve but it felt to Lanky as if they were.

Joe ran up to Cass and berated him loudly and at length, using all sorts of words that were not in the manual, something he had not had to do since the early days. Cass, looking more sheepish than shepherd-like, slunk away.

Second time they tried it, Lanky was armed: a top quality turbo-power Star Wars water pistol, or it would have been if washing-up liquid squeezy bottles hadn't been available free. Timing would be of vital importance. A jet of water up Cass's nose would not necessarily stop him if it was squirted too soon. He might simply give a shake of the head and come on again, even more determined. Too late and it wouldn't stop him either, the missile being already launched and fully committed. The one thing they had in their favour was that Cass hated water.

Lanky ran past carrying his water bottle. Joe shouted, 'Stand still or I will send the dog', Lanky took no notice as he ran around an imaginary arena, and Joe sent Cass away with a 'Hold him.' Lanky stopped and turned to face Cass, not something many people, and certainly very few police officers in that force, would have been willing to do at that range. Cass came on, ears down, tail down, galloping at full pelt in a dead straight line aiming at Lanky. When he judged the dog to be three paces away from his leap, Lanky squirted. It hit Cass full in the face, up his nose, in his eyes, everything.

The dog slid to a halt, backed away a few steps, and barked

his annoyance and puzzlement. It was the perfect stand-off except for the circling. Joe ran up to fuss him, so Cass was even more confused.

It only took a few more repeats of the exercise before Cass fully understood the message. The sight of the squeezy bottle became enough, then a raising of the hand as if with a bottle, then nothing at all.

To complete the perfect routine, Cass had to circle the criminal. This was an easy matter of curriculum revision. Joe had Cass's favourite ball, which he passed from hand to hand behind his back, and Cass went around after it. Joe tossed the ball to Lanky, who did the same. OK so far. Now they would try a stand-off but with Lanky holding the ball, and that worked well too. Cass trotted around and around, barking all the while.

Everything was going so well. Obedience was spot on, stand-off had at last made a virtue out of Cass's hatred of water, and agility was good enough if hardly the star turn. There would be agility competitions at Crufts featuring 100 mph border collies that could slip through the eye of a needle, so not a lot would be expected of a 90 lb police dog. Even so, Joe was determined to get it as near to perfection as possible, which was why he spent time on it when maybe others wouldn't have. Mac McKay came up to inspect progress with three weeks to go to the big day, and saw Cass do the long jump and stand motionless as he was supposed to do, waiting for Joe to come up beside him.

'Have you seen that, Joe?' said Mac.

'Have I seen what?'

'That little tic in his nearside back leg. Like laminitis in a horse.'

'Laminitis? Dogs don't get laminitis. I see what you mean, though.'

Cass was lifting his paw off the ground and then putting it down again, then lifting it, just an inch or a half inch, as if that small piece of ground was too hot to stand on. Joe put him over the three-foot hurdle and the same thing happened. The two men looked at each other.

'I'm not trying to be funny, Joe,' said Mac, 'but has he ever done that before?'

'Never,' said Joe, 'and I'd have noticed. I'm sure I would.'

'Have a word with the vet. No more training today. I don't like the look of it. Have you seen anything else odd about him, like dragging his feet?'

'No, I haven't. Dragging his feet? What do you mean? Not being keen? Being slow? Being backward in coming forward?'

'Like I say, Joe, go and see the vet. I'm not a vet. I'm just an old dog sergeant who's seen a lot of dogs.'

Joe took Cass home with his mind whirling. Dragging his feet? What's he talking about? At home, in the garden, Joe had a close look at Cass's paws. Nothing wrong with the front ones, nor the offside rear one, but what he saw on the other chilled him to the soul. The feeling in his stomach was what people usually call butterflies, but it was something heavy and dead rather than anything fluttery, more like cobblestones, and it was caused by pure fear.

Two of the nails on that back paw were slightly worn. He could see too, looking more closely, where the hair was thinner and shorter than it should have been. Cass had been licking his back paws a lot lately, but Joe hadn't attached any special significance to it. Cass had always liked to keep his feet clean. But that wasn't it. He'd been dragging his foot, literally, wearing away his nails and hair on the ground.

The X-ray showed the tops of his femurs to be not as round as they should have been. They were squarish, kind of square pegs in the round holes of his pelvic bone, which was what had caused his lifelong resemblance, in Biro's imagination anyway, to Jayne Mansfield going upstairs. Otherwise there was nothing to be seen. No spinal abnormalities showed up, no malformations or excessive wear and tear that could account for the abrasion on his paw. The vet had already looked at Cass's paws. Now he looked again, with a magnifying glass.

'Have you noticed any wobbliness in his walking? You know, as if he was a bit sloshed, unsteady on his feet.'

'No, nothing. Just that lifting his paw after the jumps.'

'Well, Joe, if Cass wasn't a German Shepherd, I'd say it could be several things, even including one or two you wouldn't have to worry about too much. Trouble is, with a GSD, it points to CDRM.'

'What? What's CDRM? Can you cure it?'

'Sorry, Joe, too many initials. Chronic degenerative radiculomyelopathy.'

'Radiculo… come on, doc. I'd rather have the initials.'

'The short name for it is degenerative myelopathy. What it amounts to is gradual loss of function in the hind legs through a degeneration in the nerves in the spinal column. We don't know what causes it exactly, and we can't treat it. We have nothing we can use to cure it, and all you can do is try to make life a bit more comfy, although I'm afraid that won't delay the inevitable. Some authorities say that drugs can help, and drug companies do nothing to disabuse people of that belief, but there's no way of showing that a dog with the disease would have done the same without drugs. I mean, we can't have a certain diagnosis except post mortem, so how can we...? Sorry, Joe. Hobby horse of mine.'

'So what can I do?'

'Exercise is good. All exercise. One activity that helps with muscle tone is hydrotherapy, otherwise known as swimming.'

'Swimming?' said Joe. 'Christ Almighty, you'd never get Cass swimming. For one thing he hates water beyond all hates, and for another when he gets wet he weighs a ton. If his back legs were weak he'd never get up again.'

'In which case, Joe, the disease will run its own course, slow or fast, depending on influences we don't understand. I'm very sorry, Joe. It's a bit like multiple sclerosis in people. There's no possibility of recovery. It just gets worse and worse.'

'Are you sure that's what it is?'

'Ninety-nine per cent. It's diagnosis by default. The blood sample I took won't show he has CDRM, but it will show that he doesn't have the other possibilities. So, if there's no other apparent cause, and he's a GSD, that's it. As soon as you notice any other difficulties with his hind legs, any abnormality however small, that will be confirmation.'

'How long, do you think?'

'Impossible to say. How old is he now, six and a half? Well, that's younger than most, I'd say. I'd expect eight or nine, that sort of age or a bit older. Which might be good news. He could live for several years. And he might be all right, reasonably fit and well, for quite a while yet. The only heartening thing about it is that they don't feel any pain. It's you who feels the pain, Joe, watching it. Sorry. Very sorry.'

'No point in glossing over, is there? Thanks for being straight with me. Will he be incontinent?'

'Not normally. It could happen, but only long after the time when he should have been... well, you know.'

'Yes, I know. Come on, Cass.'

As Joe watched his companion, colleague and best friend of five years jump into the back of his dog van, the tears came. How much longer would Cass be able to do that, a simple thing like jump in the van?

The answer was for quite some time, as it turned out. Cass was officially retired and went to live as the household pet at Castle Sleightholm and Joe went on the next dog-training course with his new animal, a GSD bitch called Tessa.

She was a fine dog, a short-haired one, constructed according to good breed guidelines and excellent at tracking, but no dog could ever be like Cass, as Joe soon proved when he was called late one night to the Chief Constable's house, no less. The Chief had disturbed two men trying to steal the family Range Rover from the gravel drive, one of several such in a locality of large detached houses, widely spaced. Joe began searching the gardens with Tessa and she soon indicated. There was someone there, not in the garden they were searching but the next one. Joe and dog ran to the gate in time to see two men fleeing down the road. Joe released Tessa with a very sharp 'Stand still or I'll send the dog' followed swiftly by 'Hold him' to make it clear to Tessa what was required – and not at all to warn the men, who were in no need of warning.

Tessa went off at full speed and disappeared into the darkness. Joe followed, listening for a bark, and reached an open gate into a meadow, which was where they must have gone. Still no bark. Minutes passed, then Joe heard her, giving the best bark she'd ever given. Terrific. She'd found, spoken and detained. Joe broke into a run, torch shining ahead... and there were two red eyes, which almost immediately turned into Tessa coming back, looking very happy, with her tail wagging. Found, spoken, commuted, villains gone.

'If that had been Cass...' said Joe to himself, and stopped. No point. Tonight's star prize – two car thieves to present to the Chief Constable, compliments of the Dog Handling Section – had vaporised. They tried tracking but, good as Tessa was at that skill, lost it after an hour.

For eighteen months, Joe and Julia watched Cass for signs to match the prognosis. They said nothing to the girls, only that Cass had moved into Leila's place as the family pet and Tessa was the new police dog. Every day, Julia took Cass for a walk, and for his second walk if Joe was on duty. Both of them had read the disease profile so often they knew it by heart: 'The cause is unknown. Degeneration in the dorsolateral funiculi in the white matter of the spinal cord is accompanied by degeneration in the dorsal spinal roots. An auto-immune basis for the disease has been suggested.'

As anyone would, they borrowed medical books from the library and tried to find answers on the internet. Peering through the grey matter and the white matter of the spinal cord and discarding the doc-speak of dorsolaterals, ataxia, paresis and medullated fibres, they made a list of signs to spot.

They knew the big symptom was loss of the use of the hind limbs. On the way to that were smaller signs that the dog's normal sense of positioning for feet and legs was being disturbed. That part of the brain and nervous system running the automatic side of life was being invaded.

One such sign was the foot dragging, which could rub away the skin and cause bleeding. One book said you could turn the dog's foot knuckle down, which he normally wouldn't let you do, and he wouldn't turn it back again straightaway. There would be a delay, proving that the disease was gaining more ground.

The dog would also lose control of his limbs and be unaware of it. He might cross his back legs and get in a muddle, or fall over when turning. If a back leg got itself into the wrong position, splayed out for instance, the dog would be slow to bring it back into proper line. Et cetera, et cetera.

The moment of truth came one day when an action so central to Cass's life, jumping into the back of the dog van or Joe's car, got beyond him. Joe was off duty, it was time for a walk, Tessa was already in the back of the family hatchback and Cass didn't understand. Instead of the normal back-leg powered leap, a neat and tidy manoeuvre he'd done a million times, he found himself scrabbling over the car bumper with his front legs while his back ones offered no thrust at all. Joe's instinct was to set Cass back a few paces and ask him again to do it. Instead, he looped his hands under Cass's body and lifted him in.

Cass sat, upright, eyes front as usual, as if nothing had happened – which, by his lights, was so. He attached no significance to one failed high-jump attempt, while Joe had to wait for a few minutes in the driver's seat until he was sufficiently dry-eyed to start the car. Like most police officers, Joe was an emotional character. Police training helped to control and channel those emotions, but certain things broke the dams. For Joe, one was hearing a male voice choir singing hymns.

His late father had been a member of such choirs all the years Joe had known him and, after retirement from the building trade, Dad's habit every Thursday morning had been to pick up two of his old singing pals and do a few of the village pubs. Sometimes Joe, as an eighteen- or twenty-year-old, had gone with them. They would sing 'Steal away, steal away, steal away to Jesus' when one went to the gents, and 'How great thou art' when a landlord appeared behind the bar. Now, with Dad long dead, Joe found tears would come unbidden whenever he heard that sort of music. 'All in the April Evening' on *Songs of Praise* was enough to reduce him to helpless blubber, which was one very good reason why he never watched it if he could help it.

Now, as the vet had prophesied, he was feeling a new pain, mixed with guilt and sorrow and his own futility, as his dog, blissfully unaware, became old and infirm before his eyes and long before due time.

Cass went downhill rapidly after that first failed car-jump. Walks became out of the question. He would lie in his run, barking at the sparrows that came for their crumbs but unable to chase them, barking if a hot-air balloon went over but unable to stand and defy it.

It was time. Joe knew it. He and Julia drank a bottle of wine after supper, and agreed it had to be done. Joe would phone in the morning to make an appointment. They were both weeping, and another bottle of wine helped not at all.

The sun shone on a glorious day. Joe got Cass out on the lawn and gave him a thorough brushing. The dog lay back, fully contented in the warmth of morning, as his friend and greatest admirer brushed him and brushed him again.

Cass hadn't been in the police dog van for a while, but Joe thought that it was right they should go in it. The usual vet wasn't there, but the young lady vet was very professional and sympathetic. She suggested that Joe, already crying, could leave Cass if he liked. Joe hesitated. Cass growled and showed his teeth, so that idea was dropped.

They would do it on the floor of the treatment room, so Joe knelt beside Cass and held him and stroked him while he kept growling and the vet nervously looked for a vein in a front paw. There didn't seem to be one, and Joe couldn't see anything any more through his tears, but he felt the tremor as the needle went in and his dearest old pal, born for the job he'd so loved doing, died in his arms.

EPILOGUE
FOR A DOG

But the poor dog, in life the firmest friend,
The first to welcome, the foremost to defend.

Lord Byron, 1788–1824

There is sorrow enough in the natural way
From men and women to fill our day;
But when we are certain of sorrow in store,
Why do we always arrange for more?
Brothers and Sisters, I bid you beware
Of giving your heart to a dog to tear.

Rudyard Kipling, 1865–1936

CASSIUS

The dog is man's best friend.
He has a tail on one end.
Up in front he has teeth.
And four legs underneath.
Dogs display reluctance and wrath,
If you try to give them a bath.

Ogden Nash, 1902–1971